T0208645

Human WHISPERERS

GUY D. PERKINS

authorHOUSE

AuthorHouse™
1663 Liberty Drive
Bloomington, IN 47403
www.authorhouse.com
Phone: 833-262-8899

Published by AuthorHouse 04/28/2022

ISBN: 978-1-6655-5795-5 (sc)
ISBN: 978-1-6655-5794-8 (hc)
ISBN: 978-1-6655-5793-1 (e)

Library of Congress Control Number: 2022907751

CONTENTS

PREFACE

A buddy told me I should consider writing a book.

"About what?" I asked.

"Conservation," was his reply.

I pushed it off for several years. But he was persistent, painfully persistent! I guess he thinks others should feel the pain of my inquisitive nature. Positive steps for conservation as it pertains to outdoor use of natural resources often gets complicated. The negative and positive effects move mostly via selfishness—or the fact that folks have payments to make to someone. Too bad it has to work that way. We, as humans, are here and there, and unfortunately, we want to be everywhere.

Everest leaps to mind as one example of overuse. Can we just stop climbing that peak?

See? Your first thoughts were selfish. Then you may have justified them by saying, "Nepal relies on the income."

OK, send them some cash—just go over there, sit on a bench, drink some coffee, and look up at that big mountain. The litter left from the climbing efforts boggles my mind. The fact that they have to organize cleanups tilts me even more. It's a big mountain with a small trail, all things considered, but it is no longer the Everest it once was. And maybe it is fine. I've only been there a couple times with *National Geographic*, via television, so I don't really know. Sometimes passion to do things outdoors overshadows clear thinking of potential outcomes that are not necessarily good for the resource you'll be in and around.

So, there you have one of my views on conservation. And what could have been a long, specific book full of research and examples of ecological abuse has become a question that has taken years to develop. Before we go imposing ourselves on Mother Nature, ask yourself this: "Is what I'm about to be involved in good for the resource?" We have one earth; we should consider taking care of it better.

So, with that somewhat in mind, I'm writing about dogs. Dogs are more interesting than many people. At least they are honest if nothing else. For me, they fit directly into the conservation world. And from there, I gain insight into the human race. They help shape me.

Mostly it is the error of the human partner when dogs don't reach their potential in the field—or anywhere else for that matter. I have found myself party to that guilt in many ways. We are not born dog owners, partners, and/or trainers. And while I started my days in the field of feathers without the aid of a dog, I just cannot imagine being without one while hunting upland birds and waterfowl. Helping recover game that is shot is a direct line to conservation. Experiences with dogs in the field have helped me sort through several of life's folders. The trick is to learn to listen to your dog.

This book will focus primarily on sporting dogs, mostly ones I have partnered with since I know those best. Some variance is allowed for the breeds that are included in their so-called specific breed function. For example, a dog for waterfowling will not always be a Lab. If you and your dog have hunted with us, and I fail to mention it, don't take it personally. If I didn't specifically follow along behind your pooch, then it is hard to offer accurate firsthand observations. However, I believe you will find some similarities in my dogs and yours. Your stories have indeed contributed to this writing.

If hunting bothers you, then you most likely won't find any interest in this writing. But, hey, what if you could better understand someone who chooses to hunt? What if you better understood an activity that was a necessity that allowed humankind to survive? What if you learned the value of wildlife? Well, then you have learned something. What would be wrong with that? I've certainly learned from both nonhunters and anti-hunters in my experiences in and around wildlife.

INTRODUCTION

If you have never been part of "dog partnering" and are looking to become involved, let me be brutally honest. Maybe I can save you some money and heartache—and save a dog some frustration. Make sure you search deep and long in your head and heart. Let some time pass. Do some more research and decide if you deserve a dog and can handle one. Part of the focus of this writing is to aid you in that decision.

You have the right to express your opinion as to what a responsible companionship would be. I will be expressing mine. Most likely, in some cases, we will both be right—and both be wrong. The following thoughts in this book are mine. I've spent fifty plus years around and observing dogs. I still learn from dogs every day. I also learn from humans, who are in the clan of "dogdum." (Don't google it—I made it up).

It took me years to finally understand what Bob Barker was expressing as host *of The Price is Right*. To this day, I'm still not sure if he had a canine close in his life. At the end of the show, he'd say "Remember to have your dogs and cats spayed or neutered." His comment offended me for years, and I wasn't sure why. Then, one day, it just clicked. I don't remember the day or the situation that caused the click, but it all boils down to responsible partnerships. You never really "own" a dog, and it has begun to bug me when I hear it or when I use the expression.

I'm going to try to convince you that your four-legged partner that you might take hunting is more than a tool. Dogs are not yard ornaments either. I've always had difficulty when a dog is kept staked and chained, especially if there is not cover present. Well, it's a guard dog, you say? Really? What is it guarding—that ten-foot circular area of dirt where the chain allows it to circle the stake? Oh, it's the bark that keeps the crooks away—and every neighbor awake for five homes in all directions. You'd bark too if I chained your butt outside in all sorts of weather.

Maybe you live in Alaska and a big part of your life centers on sled dogs. Tethering those dogs could be, and most likely is, a part of responsible partnering. The tethering might be a necessary part of the training exercises and safety for the dogs and other creatures. Again, research, soul-search, and decide on a plan as you go into the canine partnering. And if you do the evaluation and still miss the mark, leave yourself an out that is good for all involved, especially for the dog. In the following chapters, you will see that I used, or was party to, a couple of side-door exits.

There is a big responsibility that comes with keeping a dog. Let's do a little math. A thirty-three-pound bag of dog food at this writing is thirty-five to fifty dollars. Manufacturers sometimes crack me up. They don't raise the price; instead, they just hide the cost increase with a smaller bag. Really? If the dog has some kind of health glitch, you can add twenty dollars a bag. For a fifty-pound dog, that supply of food may last a month.

Vet bills, depending on where you live, are going to run a hundred to two hundred dollars every six months just for minimum shots. A little bad luck with the dog ingesting something it shouldn't, and you could add another five hundred dollars just for starters—give or take a couple bucks. Been there, done that.

If you decide on a vacation and can't take the dog, add a hundred dollars a day minimum for a dog-sitter. Last I checked, I couldn't find insurance for that cell phone the dog disassembled or the new couch that became the dog's new chew toy. Then there is the big one: a bite. They are animals, and even the best-tempered animal can have a weak moment and lash out. Bite the wrong person, and a good lawyer might get most of what you own.

The same friend who asked me to start writing about conservation is missing a portion of his ear because the dog thought it was a chew toy when he was a toddler. I'd like to think my experiences with dogs would allow me to protect myself if I was attacked by a dog, but I'd prefer not to have to physically wrestle one that meant business. With one dog that was less than seventy pounds, I might stand a chance. With two dogs, the odds would be in their favor. I've had a couple instances where giving the command "no" was enough to ward off what could have been a perforating situation. I wouldn't call those dogs vicious—more like territorial and nervous.

I am defiantly not a "dog whisperer," but I have always been lucky enough to live in a place where I could be part of a dog's life. There was always enough room to work with my hunting companions either out the back door or on a short drive. A golf course now stands over some of the best pointer-training pheasant haunts I used to practice pointers in.

If a house dog partner is all you need, then there you go. That effort will have its own set of adjustments. My nephew has a Great Dane named "Tiny." I can't quite wrap my head around it being a house dog, but he has worked to make it work for all involved. That is the key. A well-mannered and functional dog is work and often reflects the human's commitment and abilities.

Recently, I was discussing age with a friend. I'm not even sure how it came up or the exact topic that fostered it. He asked me how long I thought I had to live. I'm not sure he was aware of how much thought I often give that topic. I have dodged death a couple times in my life. Bullet placement was one lucky zig and zag. Getting shot is something to avoid.

At the young age of fifty, I was able to head off the possibilities of a heart attack before it became one. While bird hunting with a friend, and our four-legged partners, I was dragging along more than usual. All fall, I'd felt a tad off. The effort brought to the forefront that I might need to have my heart checked. I did within the next couple of weeks, and I was a candidate for the "triple B." Nice catch, but it wasn't without complications. The miracle workers brought me back for more earthly punishment of those who I'm around. My wife has not fully forgiven me for my antics in intensive care. Prior to the surgery, they told me I'd be unable to speak with the tubes in when I woke up and to not be alarmed. I was set to "male through it" and prove them wrong. Nope—that wasn't going to happen. Within seconds of waking up and discovering my inability to speak, I motioned for paper and a pencil. I'm sure my wife was looking for the "love you, honey, glad to be back" note. Instead, I scratched out, "How are the dogs?" I'll blame it on the meds.

My answer to the longevity-of-life question was this: "About a dog and a half." You do the math. I'm sixty as of this writing. Spring has sprung, and the bumpers are bouncing more often. The rooster tail of mud shot from under the pads of a young sonic yellow Lab gathering ground to get to them is observed. I never tire of the scene. So, maybe two or two and a half dogs is a better answer.

ACKNOWLEDGMENTS

To my father and his never-quit example. I am forever grateful for his encouragement and interest in my outdoor enthusiasm. To my mother, who couldn't understand why I laid out of college in the fall to guide and hunt. (I'm pretty sure I didn't tape the toilet paper roll scope on the toy gun myself, Mother).

Dad passed away while sitting atop his favorite wood-splitting block. The sun was warm there in late March. He often sat there to enjoy a cup of coffee midday. He'd been in pain for years, but he never complained in front of me—if he did at all. I missed our conversations, but I knew he was encouraged by where I had lit in life.

Mom died in her sleep. Unfortunately, it was inside an assisted living center, but it was only a short distance from what my brother turned into her favorite fishing hole. Prior to her illness, on her eightieth birthday—at least thirty years away from fly-fishing—I took her to the ranch. Using my fly rod, she built a loop and then shot the fly tight to the grassy bank with the precision and grace she reflected in all other areas in her life. It was amazing—and the fish all paid!

Dad and me

Mom and me

Chapter 1
AN INTRODUCTION TO DOGS

THAT IS A LOT OF dog! Yes, a Norwegian elkhound is a sporting dog. Duke was huge, at least to this eight-year-old boy. Why we had him, I don't know. We had a few elk where we lived, but it was illegal to chase them with a dog. Anyway, it's really a moose dog—and some Scandinavians refer to moose as elk. We had a big yard for him to run in, and he had a comfortable doghouse roughly the size of a small shed. He was a beautiful dog. Unfortunately, he liked to dig, and my mom liked to build flower gardens. Those two things just were not compatible. Duke ended up at my uncle's house where he had way more room to run and excavate in the acres of farmland around him. As I recall, he found chickens to be fair play, and that is about the last I recall of Duke.

My parents both grew up around agriculture. My mother lived her early years in a gem of a place called Dingle, Idaho. Dogs were a part of the Lewis brothers' farming operation. They were not sporting dogs. They were farm dogs, so you could say my mother had some knowledge of dogs. My father spent many of his years in and around the same small farming community, and his father was hired out to run a local cattle operation. Jig was the name of a dog I recall him talking about. Jig was a "working dog," as the American Kennel Club now classifies them, but my bet is there was no pedigree following Jig around. I guess my folks came to the dog clan through heritage or habit. They both left the farm and moved to town to pursue lines of work other than agriculture. Dogs, I guess, were just natural for them—something needed to complete their new lives.

My parents were all about the outdoors as a pastime. Weekends were spent hunting, fishing, camping, and "wood getting" (as they called supplementing the oil furnace). They didn't involve dogs in their hunting. Really, it was the TV program *The American Sportsman* that showed me dogs could be used to find and retrieve feathered game, along with *Outdoor Life* magazine, which was a staple in every home in my town in those days.

By the time I was ten, I had become a seasoned two-legged field pooch. I prided myself on marking and recovering a downed bird. One particular goose hunt is forever seared into my mind. I had a showdown with a wounded goose. The event went south as the goose decided attacking me was a way to get even. Some additional "4 chill" from my neighbors 12-gauge ended the traumatic ordeal. It was possibly then that I hatched the idea of giving up my spot as rover in the goose blind.

So, Biff entered our lives. I don't recall the selection process or if I was the one who whined enough that we needed a hunting dog that Biff was brought to the yard. He was there in the mix. I could see that he'd be challenged on the waterfowl deal because he was maybe twenty-five pounds wringing wet. And no one thought about the fact that he would need training. He was a cross of something. I heard the word "spaniel" in there, so I figured we must be good for birds. I thought bird dogs just *were*. Boy, was I wrong. Biff, by natural selection, I guess, started to pick it up just by being there.

We lived for mid-September and the sage grouse season. I'd been walking behind my parents for years, watching those gray bombers explode from the sage, and I couldn't wait to carry a gun so I could shoot my own. It was problematic from time to time to find a downed bird, especially if it was just winged. Those turned into hawk and coyote food. Biff put an end to that grocery donation. While he couldn't pick one up to bring it, he'd stand by it until we spotted him. And he developed a nose to get the ones we'd have walked past into the air for a shot.

Biff, unfortunately, bit one of my small relatives. The doghouse became vacant after that. I've always thought that incident to be a bit odd, in that Biff was in *his* house—and it was the child who crawled into the house and was pulling Biff out for whatever reason. It was a "leave me alone" kind of bite, but still, it was a bite. And maybe it was that event that put me on the path of working to be a responsible dog host and a responsible parent of children. The verdict is still out on that one, but I *am* overprotective.

By my second hunting season, at the ripe old age of thirteen, I became exposed to "real" hunting dog blood: German shorthaired pointers! Heidi belonged to our sitter's husband, Vern. My brother and I grew up latchkey kids. My mother and father both worked. Dad was a railroader and was gone a few days at a time. Mom left by seven, so Elaine would sometimes help get us out the door to school—and then we'd show up at her place after school until Mom could pick us up. Heidi was imported all the way from Germany, which is where Vern and Elaine's kids were working in the military. They shipped the dog to Vern for his birthday. He built a really neat kennel for the dog. Bear Lake, Idaho, was known for long, long, cold winters, and a shorthair just doesn't have a lot of cold-fighting coat on it. The doghouse connected from the kennel to inside the garage, and the house portion was warmed with a light.

I loved feeding and playing with the dog. I couldn't wait to go "chicken hunting"—*chicken* being local slang for sage grouse—next fall behind her.

But there was an oversight. Vern and I just thought a "hunting" dog was born built and ready to hunt. After all, the breed was "pointer." And we would have been about one-tenth right. The pointer part is in there, but you have to bring it out and help hone it. That first chicken hunt as more of a rabbit chase than anything else. I didn't know how we'd ever shoot a chicken when Heidi was out front most of the time at a hundred yards or better—and a jackrabbit didn't hold for a point. It sure was frustratingly good fun to watch her chase them up and over the ridge. The more the dog yipped, the faster she and the rabbit would go. She always put a few birds in the air, but they were mostly at the edge of rifle range.

My cousins down the street had a Brittney spaniel. The dog's name escapes me. It could hunt for its food bowl, but that was about it. One friend kept a spaniel-Lab-something-or-other, Snowball, who chased tennis balls. Another friend had a "pure" black Lab, who hunted shade. None of them hunted game with dogs. Two of the three friends hunted, so it was a quandary for me as to why no one hunted their dogs other than when they escaped the yard.

The spring of my fourteenth year, my parents were putting in a chain-link fence to replace the board fence. There was my chance: building materials! I overtook the southeast corner of the yard and started the floor to the kennel and the house, using lumber from the fence. The new fence would give me two walls to the kennel, and I'd hope for leftover chain-link for the rest. After two days, it was obvious to my parents that I wasn't stacking lumber for future use.

I was hammering away when the toe of a well-worn Red Wing work boot came into view.

"What are you building?" he asked.

Without lifting my head, I blurted out, "Building a kennel!" With the other dogs' poor history, the field wasn't exactly open for another dog. I had to go at it strong.

"And what are you going to put in there?"

"A dog," I replied.

"And where will you get this dog from?" He was now on point. Would I flush wildly or hold?

And so with the anxiety of Ralphie and his desire for a Red Ryder BB gun in the movie *A Christmas Story*, I fired back. "Browning Mountain View Kennels in Ogden, Utah. She is half paid for, and we can pick her up in a couple weeks," I said. Then, I held my breath.

Dad walked away saying nothing. I'd take that as a tie! Then my mother's shoes showed up. She was running the financials, bean counter that she was. She loved hunting sage chickens more than life itself, and losing one that was wounded was almost death to her. I had already found the chink in the anticipated adult discussion and had saved enough money for the dog. That Mom would get to see her sister in Ogden was frosting on the cake. It was game on.

I knew that my parents had bought in fully a few days later when the gate for the kennel showed up.

Chapter 2

DOLLY DOG

THERE WAS NO GOOGLE SEARCH when I started my efforts to get a dog that would help me hunt. Face and book were still two different things. *Outdoor Life* magazine had a few kennels listed in the back pages, but they were long drives east to get to them. Browning Mountain View Kennels had nothing to do with the brand Browning, the outdoor gear and firearms manufacturer. Frankly, I have forgotten how I found them. I do know I used a phone that hung on the wall and had a rotary dial. Most likely, a cousin in Ogden found me the phone number.

The kennel owner had assured me that both parents were hunting dogs. They both spent time in the field helping hunters find and take birds. There were no papers on Dolly, as in the AKC-registered papers of a pure bloodline following. The American Kennel Club thing was a bit of a mystery to this fourteen-year-old anyway. If the owner of the kennel told me Dolly's parents' breed, I don't recall. All I heard was that both parents hunted—so I'd take it from there. Over her lifetime, I was left to guess what was inside that hide. Maybe the mystery was part of the fun. I finally settled, years later, that she was either a Golden retriever/Lab cross, Lab/Irish setter, or Flat Coat/Lab. Whatever she was didn't matter. She was mine. Later, I would learn that we truly were each other's.

She was black as coal, a fuzzy little gal, with two little shiny marks on her head staring out at me. The man handed her to me, and the learning curve began. I would learn the importance of that first stare and eye contact. She wanted out from the man's arms and into mine. I paid my hard earned eighty dollars, which covered housing and shots, thanked the man, and left.

I'd set up a box in the back seat of the car for the ride home. That effort lasted long enough for her to crawl out the second time and onto my lap. It was a two-and-a-half-hour ride home. She slept on my lap, and I just stared at her. In those days, there was still pheasant habitat along the route as we drove through northern Utah along Highway 89. I thought, *Maybe she'll get to hunt there someday.* Mostly she was going to chase grouse and waterfowl. Even with the best efforts of the local rod and gun club, pheasants never took hold in the Bear Lake Valley. The habitat just wasn't right to fight off the brutal winters.

At home, Dolly had a huge, newly fenced yard to romp in. I set her down, and she immediately pooped on the lawn.

"Clean it up," was my parents' comment.

It had barely smashed grass before it was scooped up and deposited in the back corner of our large garden out the back gate. That corner eventually became the dog's go-to place. Poo management is a big deal. Think through it—and have a plan. It isn't the community's responsibility to pick up your dog's poo! Hunters, it isn't another parking lot or trailhead user's responsibility to pick up after your dog. If they bomb the parking lot, get it out of the way! I don't mean to pick on one user group, of which I'm one, but it truly is a part of outdoor manners.

What you feed your dog dictates your dog's health and the ease of poo management. If the output is consistently sloppy, then so is the input. Consider changing food brands until you find something that gives the dog a firm stool. Stool is urban language for poo, and poo is polite verbiage for "dog shit." You will have better results with cleanup if it is firm poo—and the dog will be doing well.

Dolly soon became a member of the family. Her travel boundary expanded into the house, the front seat of the car, and even a shady spot in the flower bed. Mom was slipping—I think it was the chicken thing. I credit my dad for the soft mouth Dolly had. For those who may not know what "soft mouth" means, it is the dog's ability to carry a bird without chewing or biting the edible parts of the bird. There is nothing more annoying than a dog that eats the bird on the way to your hand.

Dad no longer was directed by a schedule of being at work and had time to put into Dolly's training. He lost his leg in a train accident when I was twelve. I'd been able to carry a gun to hunt with Dad and Mom since the fall when I was twelve. The next summer brought changes to our outdoor lives that I'd never dreamed I'd be faced with. All my anticipations for an outdoor family lifestyle were dashed, stomped, scrambled and rearranged.

Dad developed a new morning ritual. When the weather allowed, which was most days, he'd sit on the back porch steps and have a cup of coffee. His peg leg could be stretched out as comfortably as possible there. Dolly—and, later, a couple of other dogs—would share that space with him.

A set of leather gloves always accompanied my dad. I used bumpers to teach fetch, but Dad used the gloves. And since there were two gloves, Dolly was introduced early to multiple retrieves. It was inevitable that "find 'em" would be introduced. Dad got a kick out of getting out back or around the side of the house and asking Dolly to "find my gloves," which he accidently, on purpose, had left somewhere. At first, I wasn't happy about that nifty trick because the things didn't have feathers on them, they were not a bumper, and it was outside of "training time." I eventually came around when I introduced two bumpers. (Geez, we humans are, as the British say, "thick" sometimes). Training doesn't always have to be regimented, and it can be transferable to the field.

There are many great dog stories around us. And with technology expansion, we get to hear about many of them now. However, there are no stories like the stories brought to you via your pooch. If you look deep enough through them, you can sometimes solve a query of life. Dogs are not in it to intentionally make your life a challenge—like some humans seem to be. A dog just wants to do what pleases you and them. They are built by you. If they are a dope, you most likely didn't get the info and learn the program to help them. I think the tech world states it as "garbage in, garbage out." That is about all I heard in my college computer science class. I paid good money for that one important sentence. Once in a while, your dog just does something that drops your jaw! Regardless of your programming, it is something they just come up with on their own—and you really can't take the credit for it beyond providing food and quarters.

My parents had a rental property in Alpine, Wyoming. One of the renters had a ninety-pound yellow Lab named Stony. He had taught this dog to hold a book of matches on his nose and not move until he was told. I thought that was pretty cool. Of course, I had to try to up it a notch. It didn't take Dolly long to learn that she'd get that dog cookie if she just held still. The word "chow" would allow her to drop it. But she didn't just drop it. She would move her nose out from under it and catch it before it fell an inch. The speed was incredible and jaw-dropping. To my knowledge, there is no way to teach a dog to dive underwater. I've had three that did.

In the field, this little forty-five-pound pooch constantly amazed me. I honestly don't recall her first retrieve on a bird. There were many flushes and retrieves. My friends and I were teenagers, and that meant limits were the end of the hunt. We were on that time line of developing a sportsman, where for reasons only known to the psychology crowd, limiting out was important. Two friends in a duck hole was fun for Dolly. Three friends were just seven more trips of fun.

As we were hunting a flood pasture one morning, the temperature had dropped to the teens. I was standing in hip boots in water that was just below my knees. After the first few bunches of ducks, there was a lull. Dolly was sitting behind me on a lump of vegetation, so she could be out of the water, and I kept hearing a funny sound behind me. I'd turn to look at her, and she'd just look at me. When I'd turn away, I'd hear it again. I finally figured out what I was hearing. Her teeth were chattering. I knew I was warmer from the knees down than I was from them up. I had Dolly come sit in the water by me. The water went up to her shoulders. The chattering stopped. The ducks started again, and the rest was limits. It is unnatural for a dog to want to sit in water. We had never practiced it—she just understood it.

Neoprene vests for dogs didn't come along until after they were used in waders for humans, and there is still a question if vests help the dogs stay warm. Some schools of thought are that the dog can't shake to stand up its hair, which is the natural insulator when it's on end. Other folks believe a dog should be able to roll in the snow to help dry off and help stand the hair up.

As we move forward, I will continue to write about things that make your dog comfy. Comfy dogs are happy dogs. They will work harder and longer with comfort involved. Part of the comfort is also intended for the safety of your dog. I know I frustrate some folks I hunt with because I worry so much about my dogs' comfort. No bird to bag is worth hurting your loyal companion. If comfort helps stretch another year of good life out of them, then I'll pack the heater. This next situation lives strongly in my mind today, and it is with me every time I go afield.

It was late November, and a high school pal and I were jumping ducks up off some warm open ponds. We walked along the Bear River to get to them. As rivers go, most of the Bear River is fairly tame. You would be bored if you are looking for a whitewater experience. In some part of the river, during the fall, you would bottom out in a kayak. High banks can be an access issue down to the water in some areas. In the Bear Lake Valley of southeastern Idaho, the river meanders back and forth without much current at all. Slow places the waterfowl like are usually frozen over by mid-November, and most of the birds have been driven south by the snow and cold.

We'd just rounded a corner and were not far from the vehicle when a couple ducks flew past. Without really giving the location any heed, I toppled one. It fell into a section of the river that had iced over. There was an open hole about fifteen feet across and sixty feet long. It fell toward the upper end, and before I knew it, Dolly was in there with the bird in her mouth. She made the upstream edge of the ice hole, but with the bird in her mouth, she couldn't lift a back leg high enough to catch the edge of the ice. There was ice for thirty yards before it opened up for some distance below the hole.

I only had on hip waders and was not familiar with the water depths right there. I knew the ice wouldn't hold me to give aid. All I could do was watch in horror as she tried and tried to get that back foot up.

"Leave it!" I Called.

That was not getting her to drop the bird. The slight current most likely wasn't helping her, but it was enough to push her hind end up toward the surface as she clung to the ice with her front legs. The duck kept her from pulling more with her front legs. It most likely was only half a minute before a claw of her hind leg grabbed the ice edge and leveraged her up

9

and out, but it felt like hours. I wanted to puke! In hindsight, I had made several mistakes. I should have been more aware of my surroundings. I should have said, "No," "Sit," or "Stay." I could have taught her not to break until I gave the command, but that kind of goes against how she was geared and hunted upland birds. It did teach me to pay better attention to the field safety situation. For the most part, my dogs and I just don't do ice.

I'd worked with Dolly to be a versatile dog; she would hunt upland and waterfowl birds. Our chicken-hunting efforts, which I'd so wanted to roll Dolly into, changed because of my father's physical challenge. Sage chickens are built to be walked up to. In other words, you covered the county to find them on foot. They did frequent certain habitats that took the looking at certain times of the day into a smaller geographic area.

My father became the taxi driver, dropping us off and picking us up in the wide expanse of sagebrush that the birds called home in southeast Idaho. It was never the same though, and I know it wasn't the same for my mother. She'd keep a good face, and we'd forge ahead.

Dolly would hunt close, and we could always tell when she was "birdy." Every hair on her body was on the move, and her nose was tight to the ground as she huffed and puffed the scent. Our hearts would race because we knew it was going to happen. There is nothing like the sound of one of those "gray bombers" hitting the air. And if ten get up at a time, the challenge is to come back to earth, focus on one, and get it shot. Early in the season, a group may just sail a couple hundred yards and light after you disturbed them. Two days into the season, they may sail for a mile before they set down again. They are notorious walkers—and you most likely will not recover a wounded one without a dog. If both legs are intact, they can walk and cover the ground at an amazing pace. They can also hide.

On one particular day, we'd gotten into a bunch and shot four. We had recovered three that had fallen close, but one was a glider and sailed across the draw. I had watched it hit the ground and could see it. In a moment, it was up and walking. I called Dolly and headed down and across to where the bird had been. I was pretty sure it would continue to walk uphill, and I cut out a bit ahead of it.

When we got to where Dolly should have picked up the scent track, she didn't act interested at all. So, we started a back-and forth-pattern down toward where I had last seen the bird. When I got to my best guess of where it had hit the ground, I started looking for feathers in hopes of getting Dolly on the scent.

Dolly? Where is she now? She was just below me a second ago. I called to her. I whistled—nothing. I stepped to my left, and she was twenty feet away, staring down a badger hole. *Great,* I thought. *She is either on a rabbit, which would tick me off, or the hole has an occupant.* I'm not a badger fan. They have attitude. They are nasty little critters.

I walked up to Dolly and unloaded my side-by-side shotgun. I wasn't going to reach down the hole. I carefully slid the barrel about a foot into the hole until I felt it hit something. The something felt soft and pliable. There wasn't a growl. Dolly just kept staring in the hole. So being the adventuresome person I am, I told Dolly to fetch it up! She worked at it, but she could only get in far enough to come out with feathers to confirm it was the bird. I reached in and was able to get a leg and extract the bird from the ground. Had it not had a broken wing, I may have considered releasing it. Without Dolly, the bird would have gone to waste.

Yes, we liked eating sage chickens. It's just a matter of how you prepare them. Young birds fry up pretty well. The ones we called "ridge runners," older birds, were usually males that required some creative cooking. They were not anything a Dutch oven couldn't solve. As my interest in cooking expanded, I discovered that a soaking marinade would tender game up a bit. A favorite soak is in milk overnight in the refrigerator. You can get creative from there.

Pheasant was one of those birds I was introduced to by *American Sportsman*. In my mind, I had somehow conjured up that a real bird dog hunted pheasant. The Bear Lake Rod and Gun Club had released a few birds into the Bear Lake Valley, but they just didn't take hold. A few were around, very few, but the habitat just wouldn't sustain them. The predator populations didn't help either. Fox and coyote populations were through the roof since poison to control them had been outlawed. There just were not enough trappers in the valley to keep the numbers in check.

The first pheasant I saw in the field blew into air from the reed patch that surrounded the pond I was about to hunt ducks on. It was possibly the last remaining pheasant in the valley. Man, that unscrewed me! The cackling commotion and colors glistening in the sun as it worked to straighten the curls from its tail and create distance between us are pretty much tattooed in my mind. The closest pheasant that was legal to hunt was westward about an hour in Franklin County, Idaho. My father and a neighbor had hunted them there before and were able to walk up a couple every trip. Having a dog to root them up and help recover them should help the adventure.

Our first outing was on a Saturday in October. West of Preston, Idaho, we found a place that had what looked to be likely cover. We knocked on the door of a farmhouse that was adjacent to it. After getting permission to hunt into the draw, we went. There were enough birds in those days that most cover held a bird or two. Three of us had limits in about an hour, and I was so overwhelmed with the emotions of just being on a pheasant hunt that I can't remember anything about Dolly's contribution other than she brought a couple birds to hand. She was covered in burrs—burrs like I'd never seen before—and they were embedded deep in her hair. Dolly's coat resembled more of a setter or a golden retriever than the tighter Lab nap. Cleaning her up usually was an hour-long process after she had worked on them herself during the hour-long drive back over the hill to home. She didn't like them any more than I did. She got pretty good at grooming herself.

The next year, we learned of the pheasant heaven in Burley, Idaho. It was another two hours west. We learned of it thanks to one of my cousins who married a pea farmer from there. It was an amazing place. There were so many birds that you could hunt them in the hayfields where they often rested during the day. Burley would usually cut two crops, and the third crop may or may not make it to maturity before fall. So many fields had a ten-inch stand. For some reason, the birds just liked hanging out in them during the day.

Our relative said we had not really seen anything for birds. Really? Maybe we hadn't. The next day, we drove southwest thirty minutes to the small town of Oakley. Through the relative, we had secured a place to hunt there as well. It was a small draw, maybe fifty yards across and two hundred yards long, full of great-looking cover. We started in there with Dolly and her year-old pup, Star. Immediately, they got birdy. I would learn how well pheasants can run. Birdy dogs? No birds getting up? It was a quandary.

When we got to the bottom of the draw, toward some thicker cover, the place just blew up! If I said a hundred birds got up, I'd not be fibbing!

If I said we shot limits, I would be. As I recall, they got up long. Even the couple that were close got a pass or a miss—let us say pass, shall we?—because we couldn't close our mouths to cheek the stock of the gun! I'd never seen anything like it—not even on television. *American Sportsman?* Who needs it!

On one of these trips to Burley, I learned at Dolly's expense just how nasty a direct battery-run hot wire, meant to keep large cattle in, could be on a dog. I was pretty sure the wire was hot (full of electrical current). Dolly and I were walking a ditch bank, and I was looking for a place I could crawl under the wire. I saw a sag in the wire I could step over about the time Dolly got to it. Her panting open mouth caught the lower wire, and it laid her over.

When I got to her, her eyes were glazed—and she was flinching. I had no idea what to do.

Luckily, she came out of it in about ten seconds. It took her another twenty seconds to stand. She wobbled for a bit, and then she stopped and looked at me. Her eyes were clearer, and they seemed to ask, "What the $#%&* was that about?"

I felt terrible. We do hot wires with way more caution now.

Chapter 3

STAR

S TAR WAS FROM DOLLY'S ONLY litter of pups. Dolly was a good mother. I'll later cover my opinion on breeding dogs. That opinion has been changed and shaped over the years. So, look forward to that in an upcoming chapter. For now, we will just cover it by saying Dolly was a good dog.

According to Mr. Parker's high school biology class, I deducted if I could find a good mate for Dolly with good traits, we could maybe come up with another almost Dolly. Good dogs live way too short. So, that is how Star came to be. He was a purebred eighty- pound Black Lab without papers. He hunted a few ducks and had a good disposition. without papers. He was Star's other parent. Star was about as laid back as a dog can be. She became my brother's dog. My brother Rod was five years my junior. He named her Star for the one dime-sized patch of white hair on her chest. She was sixty pounds with the coat of a Lab. Dolly was forty-five pounds. Star picked up the extra size and coat from her father.

Star was easy to train. I think she picked up some of it from watching Dolly. My dad spent a bunch of time with both dogs, and there was always some kind of lesson going on. Three things got Star wound up: truck rides to the canyon to get wood, birds attempting to get away, and softball games. Yup, softball games. My brother played a lot of softball, and our parents—and the dogs—were his biggest fans. The dogs would sit on the toolbox of the old '71 Chevy pickup and watch the ball pitched in and hit out! The dogs' heads turned like synchronized swimmers.

They'd ride in the back of the truck empty to the canyon to get a load of wood and then lie on the top of the toolbox all the way home. They didn't want to be in the cab. These rides in the truck were slow—not on an interstate or even a heavily traveled state road. It's what dogs did back then, and to some extent, it's what they still do. I'd never heard of a dog crate in the seventies. I started to notice them in the eighties. And my opinions of dogs riding loose in the back of a vehicle have also changed over the years.

If you're a farmer with a flatbed, and you are riding around on the farm with your dog hanging on the edge, great—but don't bring them to town that way. One, it appears that the safety of your dog doesn't matter to you. And if it were to fall off, and someone swerves to miss it and runs their vehicle into someone or something, you might be liable. It might fall under the securing your load law. I've seen some great livestock dogs in my time. I used to help the local cattlemen's association gather and turn out cows on the summer forest pastures. Not that I was any real help, but it was more to help me train my mustangs for mountain duty. Why would you let your best help ride somewhere they may get hurt? Getting kicked by a cow is an occupational hazard, but falling off the back of the truck and into the street is something you can control. In my opinion, there are still too many dogs riding loose in the backs of open vehicles.

If there was a descriptive word for Star and her manner, it would be "lumpty-dump." Scratch me? I'm good! If there was a bird involved, then it was like, "Hey, where is Star—and who's dog is that?"

I first saw that transformation just out of Burley, Idaho, on her first pheasant hunt. Someone broke the wing on a rooster, but it still had legs. It took off across a disked field (the crops were turned, and soil was worked down until it was fairly smooth). Star was hot on it. The rooster would turn sharp as Star was feathers away from securing it. Star would skid around with claws grabbing, legs digging, and dirt flying. This went on for several turns, and then from way deep, Star came in another gear. The bird couldn't out-position itself. After that event, things with feathers belonged to Star. If she could get there first, it was hers.

I wasn't around for the specific hunting adventures with Star like I was with Dolly. When I left for college, my brother and his friends utilized both Star and Dolly. I was an hour and a half away in Utah, but I came home every fall to hunt. I asked my brother to give me one good hunting story about Star for this book, but it didn't happen. Family pass—so, I'll have to tell one about him later.

Chapter 4

SHALL WE FISH?

W**HEN THERE WASN'T A BIG** game or bird season going, we spent time fishing. We had a boat, but it was hard for my father to manage with the one leg. Eventually, it was sold. He was a fly-fisherman more than he was any other style of fisherman. He could hobble fifty yards of stream while the rest of us had five hundred yards of stream, and he would still out-fish us.

Dolly and Star loved to walk beside him and just hang out and watch. The splashing of landing a trout always got them anxious, but they knew not to touch. We had learned about a small lake in Wyoming with no banks that would be easy for my father to manage. On Father's Day, a fly hatch was always on, and it created a feeding frenzy for a few hours in the mornings. The trout were browns and brookies. They were not creek-sized, but they were nice and chunky two-to-three-pounders with pink meat and outstanding table fare.

The hatch required a bit of cheating by purist fly-fishing standards. To reach the hatch, you had to change up the rod to a spin-out fit and float the fly with a bubble. The fly of the day was a Platte River special—or damsel. The fly was attached to an eight-inch dropper above a floating clear bubble that had a bit of water in it to add weight for casting distance. I've seen some fair to middlin' line haulers in my life, but I never saw one that could lay the fly out the distance needed to reach the hatch from the bank. Float tubers were few in those days, but the few we did see seemed to prefer to "sink" the fly with weighted line and fish after the hatch was over for the day.

Oftentimes, we'd catch a fish shy of our limit and then continue to catch and release until the hatch played out. Dad had played a brookie that was full of fight a little longer than usual, and the fish was not doing well on the release. The fish was far enough offshore that we couldn't wade to try to get him back. Wasting wildlife has never been an acceptable practice for us, and this fish would finish my father's limit for the day. It nagged at him that it looked like it would die and not be utilized; therefore, it would be wasted.

A float tuber could have netted it for us, but they had all disappeared. Dolly, as usual, had been hanging around and watching all the proceedings. The next thing I heard was, "Dolly, fetch!" Away she went.

I thought, *This will be interesting.*

She swam to the fish and bumped it with her paw, and it went below the surface. She swam around in circles looking for it. I'd seen her reach under the water to catch diving ducks, but this was a fish, which she'd always been taught to leave alone. The fish surfaced again, and she attempted to grab it—but down it went. She dog-paddled and continued to look. On the next miss, she disappeared below the surface as well!

When she came up, the fish was squarely in her mouth—and she was headed for the bank. Had it been today, the cell phone cameras would have been out of everyone's pockets to capture the event. We used cameras a bunch outdoors, but in those days, nothing was handy. We have six witnesses that will swear it, and we have the pictures in our minds. It was nothing short of amazing, and the fish didn't have a mark on it. I guess if there was any question at all, it would be this: "Did she need a license?"

If you take your dog fishing with you, it is important to teach them to leave the fish bait alone. They will have a bit of a tendency to want to grab it as it swings past them prior to the cast. And when it's baited, that is food for the dog as far as they are concerned. The last thing you want is your dog swallowing a hook or getting a lure in the lip. With pups, I sometimes make the comment that they think their name is "No." It is a word they need to know. No means No! Lay off it and leave it alone!

When you have your dog around areas where people fish, watch them closely or leash them. Don't let them go off sniffing around. Finding a baited hook creates a huge risk. A place I frequent for waterfowling and fishing has a boat dock that people fish from, and they leave baited hooks lying around all the time. Nowadays, in most areas where there are people and facilities, you are required to leash your dog. That is not required in this place, but leashing is the only way to have complete control of your dog. It only takes a second for them to eat something that they—and you—will not care for later.

I'm lacing this writing up with dog safety as it chronologically came along. Later, I'll recap some do-and-don't considerations on their own page because it's really important to your dog and your enjoyment of the outdoor experience.

I want to cover traps, leg holds, and snares. I want to start out by saying that I am not against trapping. Trapping helped shape this country. As with a lot of things outdoors, trapping was overdone in some regions of the country. It is easy to look back and find fault. In many instances, the use and abuse of a life resource came down to an us-or-them decision.

There are many areas, such as national wildlife refuges, that could use a hard-core focus on trapping, especially refuges that serve as nesting areas for our feathered friends. Predators are hard on bird nests! Know the trapping laws and what is going on in the areas that you and your dog frequent. I hunt property managed by Pacific Corporation. They use water to build electricity for us. All their access points have signs that warn that you need to get permission from them in order to trap. That doesn't mean that everyone honors the signage, but it does make me feel a bit more comfy about being able to find out what trapping activity is going on so I can remain vigilant to the practice.

One fall afternoon, when I was sixteen, we were fishing by a local bridge where we had fished in the past. As usual, Dolly was hanging around our feet. I was intent on fishing and didn't notice her wander under the bridge. All at once, there was a commotion of yipping and growling! I looked toward it and saw Dolly jumping up and down. She was hung up in something. I bolted to her to find her front paw in a number-2 leg-hold trap that was set for a bobcat or a fox.

A number-2 trap usually requires some skill to set. You can stand on the springs or be mountain man enough to bend the trap over your leg with leverage to depress the springs and open the jaws. Without thinking through it, I grabbed the springs—one in each hand—and the adrenaline allowed me to squeeze them into a depressed position to allow the jaws to open.

I grabbed the springs, and Dolly grabbed me. Luckily, I was wearing leather gloves. The trap didn't break the skin. She limped around for a few minutes and basically walked it off. I still worry about traps every time I go afield. A snare could be a worse situation because the cable loop is designed to pull tighter and hold when the captured animal fights back. Basically, the animal suffocates and passes out. The cables are usually small in diameter, but it would take a sharp, good-quality multitool or side-cutters to cut the cable. I never go in the field without a tool. Snares are usually set on fence lines on trails or runs used by predators that pass under the fences. Many states require some kind of visual marking that will allow you to know there are traps in the field.

Chapter 5
ACROSS STATE LINES

$\mathcal{Y}$OU KNOW WHAT THEY SAY about the grass being greener on the other side of the fence? It was to that end that Dolly and I found ourselves surrounded in Utah.

I'd left the country for a couple years and then returned to resume my studies at Utah State in 1980. While the human population of Utah was growing, they still had plenty of pheasant hunting opportunity in those days. The farming communities sold trespass permits that allowed you to hunt anywhere within the boundary of the community. If a landowner did not want to participate, they just posted their property with the standard fluorescent orange—and you couldn't hunt it. Other areas were posted with signage that said: "Posted hunting unit permit required." Some of the communities had pheasant raising and release project that were Boy Scout projects or church fundraisers. The money raised went to some community project. In my opinion, it was a good deal. As farming and development started to clash, the programs went away because the habitat did.

A high school classmate ended up working at the same place I did at Utah State University. He had never hunted pheasant and wanted to. Another college friend's father ran a church farm for the Church of Jesus Christ of Latter-Day Saints that was located about a fifty-minute drive southwest of Logan in an agricultural belt called Corinne, Utah. He invited us to come and hunt with him and his uncle on the pheasant opener. Dolly was living part-time with me and part-time with my folks in Idaho. The church farm didn't participate in the community hunting units. It was hunting by permission only. You just had to ask to get on. They wanted to know who was there and somewhat control the numbers for safety reasons. The back side of the property was kind of landlocked and looked like a good opportunity to avoid some of the crowding that sometimes occurred on opening day.

The season opened at 8:00 a.m. At 7:50, we were standing by a neglected acre of weed that we'd watched at least a dozen roosters land in. *Wow, this is going to be good!* At 7:55, we were surrounded by at least ten other people who had used the railroad right-of-way to gain access to the back of the property. It wasn't looking good now. It was kind of a standoff, but we had the inside of the circle. We crossed under the fence and started through the patch.

When a rooster broke, you couldn't shoot because they were flying toward someone, but the gun-carrying individuals who surrounded us didn't seem to care where the birds flew. And the shooting commenced—inward! My buddy was a defensive back in football, and he didn't have a good game unless he hit the ballcarrier hard enough to have him sit out some of the game, He was white with fear! Seriously, he wanted out—and so did I. I tried not to show panic. We decided that standing still was maybe the safest thing to do. Grouped, we could look like the "Great Pumpkin," and maybe we would reduce the opportunities to get peppered! I called Dolly to heel, and we just stood there until everyone ran out of patience and left. It truly was scary.

On that hunt, I was introduced to the pheasant hunting shorthair pointer. I use the term "hunting pointer" loosely. I never did quite catch his name. Someone was calling to him, and it went something like this: "%## *(%)$$ #$$, come here!" I thought I made out the name Buck. He looked like a "Buck," so that is what I called him. Buck was content to follow us along as a non-participating observer. The one pass he made at Dolly was met with a "Get away—I'm hunting!" So, Buck was content to continue along with us. He entertained himself by peeing on every other fence post.

He did stop to watch the pheasant pile up, which Dolly promptly retrieved. Well, at least he didn't seem gun-shy. Mostly, he seemed just bored by it all. After half an hour or so, Buck just started leaning right and faded off to the north, never to be seen by us again. It seemed that every shorthair pointer I observed in the field had this "Buck attitude" about it. Surely, they just can't be that dumb. In a few short years, I'd find the answer to that query.

We finished up with a fine collection of birds that day, and I observed Dolly giving her first point. I don't have any idea where that came from. Maybe she was just trying to show me what Buck was supposed to be about. Maybe she just felt my confusion and was trying to get my head back to the task at hand. Who knows? Maybe she was starting to slow up in her later years, showing me where it was and telling me to kick it out myself. Some things you don't teach a good dog. They just manifest themselves with no apparent reasoning behind it. And so with that in mind, this is an appropriate place to mention Spud.

Dolly and Spud spent a few outings together on Cutler Reservoir of the Bear River back in the day. The "day" being defined as the days before the crisis of bad steel shot and its crippling effect on waterfowl and the waterfowler. Nothing like the mass weight physics of lead to put a duck in the soup. I get it to some extent. Back then, I didn't get it at all. I couldn't understand why steel shot couldn't have been eased in and better developed as a product with a bit of time and tax relief for those manufacturers working to get it there. The Feds just missed it on that one, especially when comparing the filth of water happening all around them that devastated shorebirds and waterfowl that had nothing to do with lead pellets. Couple that with a CRP program that changed the flight paths of migrating waterfowl, and well … it has been messy.

Luckily, the steel shot thing got better as time went on. The conservation effort of CRP in my mind? The verdict is still out. It could use a little more thought for useful management of the program. Seems like we are missing out on a great landowner buy-in for wildlife, the general public, and sportsmen. I'm not a great gardener, but I do know that manipulation of soil does good things for the plants I'm working to bring forth. CRP sits back and does nothing but create a monostructure that helps little wildlife. I'll leave my thoughts of conservation of that program for another day.

Spud and Dolly got along great. As I'll explain in a later chapter, that doesn't always happen in the field when dogs get together on hunts. But these two got along well. They would both water retrieve. Maybe the edge went to Dolly for longer swims, but Spud had a special "stick-to-it" talent I'd never seen before or since.

We worked hard to drop ducks in the open water to help with the recovery, but once in a while, one would get into the reed cover behind us. Dolly might take a quick look, maybe grab an easy one, and then be back watching the decoys—but not Spud. She'd be back in the reeds, and she would stay there until she found the duck. We never lost one, and I'm not kidding. She partnered with my friend Dale.

Recently, Dale and I were talking about Spud while we were hunting some thick pheasant cover that challenged the four dogs helping us. We both concluded that about an hour was the longest she ever looked for a dead duck. We knew Spud had some blue heeler (cattle dog) and springer spaniel (flushing sporting dog) in her, but after that, she was a mystery. On pheasants, she'd hunt close, and she had a great nose. If we were able to call Spud off a dead bird in the brush to help with water collections, she'd just slip back into the cover and continue to search when we were not looking. You can encourage the drive to find, but I'm not sure you can teach the "stick to it" like she had.

Getting the bird to hand after you have shot it is where the "conservation" portion of the dog really comes in. If you're a hunter, you can lean toward the title of sportsman by doing your part to help with that. Help your dog by hunting places and then taking shots where the dog has the greatest opportunity to recover the bird. While hunting, nothing it totally predictable. If you have a bad experience, my advice is to work harder to avoid anything that may resemble a reoccurrence next time.

Chapter 6

CLOSING ON A DOUBLE

I T IS NOT FAIR THAT a dog's life is so short. I've finally resolved that humans live longer because we are just that dumb and need to. If you are of some religious flavor, then you might believe that you are taking that pile of life experiences to someplace after earth where you can contribute better. If you believe there is some type of a judgment of your efforts here on earth, then you better hope your dog isn't on the jury. And if they are, you better hope that they "get you" and allow a pass on your shortcomings as a dog life participant. I'm pretty sure my list is full of errors.

I'd been completely out of Dolly's hunting life for two years while I worked to pile up some of those earth assets to take to the other side. I wondered if she would remember me. I came through the back gate and around the corner of the house and saw her across the yard. I didn't say a word. She spotted me and turned and stared—and then she did the weirdest thing. She lay down and crawled ninety feet to me.

I knelt down, and when she reached me, her nose touched my outreached hand. She then went crazy, running at hyper-speed around and around the yard like she used to when we would just play! Yes, she knew me. It was emotional, but it was not nearly as emotional as her few remaining final days afield. Everything she did seemed to have some special relevance, but maybe I just paid better attention to it after my absence from the field.

I was moving on in my dog world. Dolly was now a consistent part of my folks' lives. They were all aging happily together. Big game pursuits were slowing down, but trucks, wood hauling, and fishing moved on steadily for my folks. Dolly fit right in. I had a new focus in the field of feathers: pheasant snob. I needed an appropriate partner, one of those "Buck" breed of dogs.

Life was taking on a new direction. Geographic location for college, a marriage, and waterfowling traditions flopping around in the tank were all adding to the changes. Dolly would not be happy being removed from my folks to live with us, and neither would they. Really, something was driving me to prove that German shorthair pointers were not the field issues they appeared to be.

I left the new spotted "Buck-style" dog in the kennel and took Dolly when I returned to my parents' house to go hunting ducks. Besides, the spotted dog was for the pheasant snob I wanted to become. She was a dry land dog, or so I'd been told, and I certainly wouldn't want to water down that thought, would I?

On her last hunt, Dolly and I headed for a slough below the thriving metropolis of Bennington, Idaho. It was a sloppy day with low fog rising off the warmer water. There wasn't really a plan other than to get out with Dolly on an easy hunt. The overflows would hard stop any day now, and for her efforts, her season would also end. We followed the railroad right-of-way and parked at the switch house. Dolly rode in the cab, looking alert and not reflecting the twelve years of age she was but for a little gray lip tint. We exited the truck and worked our way out into the flooded pastures off the slough. I hadn't brought any decoys because I hadn't pre-scouted. It was kind of off the cuff, and I hoped for something legally feathered to just fly by in range and fall easy for her to retrieve.

We sloshed along the ankle-deep water. The fog made it difficult to navigate. I knew that area, and for the most part, I knew where we were. I came to a little mound that brought us up and out of the water. There was just a sliver of cover available. It was a semidry spot that would be good for Dolly. In the distance, I could hear geese stirring awake as they assembled themselves to leave the water and head to the barley fields to feed. They would leave eastwardly, dang it, and not toward us.

We stood, and light began to illuminate the cloud we stood in, expanding our visibility. The smell of wet dog and marsh crept into my senses and filled my mind with recall. I gazed down at her ever-vigilant posture, ears up and head swiveling back and forth. She had been such a great dog, and she was still a great dog. She deserved inclusion as best she could offer in her later years, and it was my responsibility to help her contribute differently. The wag in her tail would define my efforts. I'd later in life find that mentality to be a shortcoming in our society. Use them up and throw them away—shame on us! It is bad enough that we produce products with that intention. That mentality leaches way too often into our human interactions.

From my partner position, I had nothing to compare her to. She was the trailblazer. I am because she was. I couldn't imagine a more perfect companion to begin to grow up with outdoors. Every dog I would have as a partner in the field, I would most likely judge them by her. I'd try not to do that, to be fair to the others that would follow, and there would be more. I would position my life and the others to honor her instead of comparing them to her. I would try to do a better job for them by working to be a better partner. I thought of her patience with me, and I would work to pass on what I had learned to them. She truly was a magical being! It would be a life project, and I was already on the edge of blowing it by leaving the spotted dog at my folks' place. I scolded myself a bit. There was no reason that spotted dog couldn't be sitting here on this short hunt other than the fact she was mostly white and visible. Hell, maybe she could help this old gal retrieve. Then again, it was an area Dolly could manage. No nasty cover or big swims. She deserved the event without competition.

Dolly focused and then stiffened, and I was jolted back to the job at hand as two winged rockets broke from the fog. They were coming head-on, one breaking left and one right. I was carrying my old Savage Fox .20-gauge side-by-side. The gun had developed a habit of almost pointing itself. I folded the one to my left and then continued to swing and collapse the one that had broken to my right. It was now behind us, fast becoming a shadow, and covered up by the fleeting fog as it climbed to outdistance the shot.

Dolly was off after the first one, returning quickly and neatly the green-winged teal to hand. She cast off the praise and lined out after the other one. It was pushing long when the pellets caught up to it. I figured we'd maybe have to spend some time trying to recover it. I'd stepped off the mound and was heading in the direction of bird and dog.

Suddenly, Dolly was there with the bird draped proudly in her mouth. She took the full rubdown at the end of this effort, and then she showered me with dog affection as she pushed the water from her coat. I decided not to ruin the perfection of the moment, and we headed for the truck. I got the old green wool army blanket from behind the pickup seat and placed it on the seat to absorb Dolly's moisture. She needed a little boost onto the floorboard, and she had climbed up onto the blanket by the time I'd come around to the driver's side.

We headed for home. Dolly was asleep beside me, and I was relishing the event—and my shooting prowess—as I mindlessly navigated the potholes along the tracks. Then it hit me! How did she know where that second bird was? She had recovered the first one in an almost opposite direction. And it was into the fog far enough that there was no way she could have seen that bird fall. The bird was stone dead when she handed it to me, so it hadn't been splashing around to give her a direction—and she was going deaf. Maybe, just maybe, she wasn't as deaf as she sometimes acted; maybe she heard the splashdown. The wind was in the wrong direction to help her scent the bird. Do age and experience just allow old dogs to practice selective hearing? I do that with my wife. I'll never know. It is a mystery of a perfect hunt.

Dolly started to come apart by spring. On a drizzly, foggy day, similar to the last day afield with her and the teal, I took her from her house inside the kennel I'd built for her as part of the plan to enter the hunting dog world. I held her on my lap as the family drove to the vet. She strained to raise her head as I carried her inside. Her breathing was slow. Cradled in my arms, with my head down toward hers, she mustered the strength to lick me once. I wouldn't lay her on the table, opting to hold her as he administered the shot that allowed her discomfort to go away. She went limp in my arms, and I watched what little life was left leave her coal-black eyes.

I held it together somewhat until I was alone and heading back home to Logan, Utah. Bena, the young white-and-brown spotted replacement dog now laid in Dolly's place with her head nestled on my hip. I was about to punish my emotions again for another twelve years. And, no, I can't stop.

Chapter 7

BECOMING A PHEASANT SNOB

ENA IS THE NORTH AMERICAN Indian name for pheasant! I was researching names from the Utah State University library, and most likely, I was supposed to be working on a paper. Oh, the life of college. Her papered name was Bena Patch Racer. Her white hair had brown splotches and lightly freckled legs. The writers had advised me that white upland game dogs are easier to keep track of in the field. And maybe that was the only reason I chose her. I don't recall looking for any other "sign" that would lead me to believe she would amount to anything in the field. I'd never hunted over her mother. And, of course, it was a gamble because, well, Buck of Corine wasn't actually on the cheer squad for the shorthair team.

With steel shot becoming the flavor of the day for shot shells in waterfowling, I was losing interest. Dolly's passing didn't help. That first steel pellet ammo was just junk! It drove many waterfowlers completely out of the exercise. Without delving too deep into the physics of it all, for those of you reading this who may not hunt, it was a matter of impact. Steel was light and lost energy quicker than lead. If I hit you with a tennis ball or a baseball traveling at the same speed, you'd be able to understand it. Late-seasoned, feathered-up ducks and geese were nightmares to bring down. The feathers stopped the penetration of the lighter pellets. Using larger shot sizes to regain the weight created more surface area on the pellet and created drag that didn't allow the pellets to penetrate. The larger-sized pellet also reduced the pellet count, which decreased the odds of a pellet striking an area to bring the bird down. Upland hunters could still use lead. Those were legit reasons for changing dog breeds, but I was really curious to find out if shorthair pointers were just dumb!

Utah had an abundance of pheasants in those days. To the north of my location, a short thirty-minute drive to Idaho, birds were also plentiful. If I played it right, I could hunt two states.

I'd gotten Bena from an acquaintance at a local archery club who swore by the breed for pheasants. That is swore *by* not swore *at*. I had experiences calling elk into bow range. Since his dog was about to have a batch of pups, we traded our talents. I'd teach him about calling elk, and he'd give me a pup. I win!

Gypsy was Bena's mother. Gypsy was truly a pheasant hunting machine. She belonged to Mark Lundahl, and they hunted pheasants like folks prepare to run marathons nowadays. Mark's grandfather had helped him with some of the training of Gypsy. For me, pointers were a new gig. I was already negatively biased until I found *Gun Dog* by Walther. I ate, drank, and applied it.

The first time Gypsy and Bena hunted together, Bena honored the first point Gypsy threw ten minutes out of the truck, and I was hooked! I can't even remember who or if we killed any birds. I just knew it was one of the coolest things I'd ever seen. Gypsy turned back into herself and just froze—from 15 mph to 0 mph. It was too quick to be measured by time. She became statue still. Bena eased toward her, and about three lengths from Gypsy, she slid into this slippery slide pose she became famous for. Time stood still, and the scene imprinted every fiber of my body.

I lived on the southwest corner of Logan, Utah, a rock toss from the county line. At that time, there were open fields, waterways, and friendly neighbors who allowed me to run and train Bena. Much of the training was done in my yard, but the actual bird thing was a two-minute walk in one direction and ten in another. Now that area is covered up with homes and a golf course. I guess golf courses are open space. With municipalities trying to figure out how to afford and manage public golf courses, maybe they should consider using it as a pay-to-use dog park in the off-season. Poo in your spikes come spring? Sorry. It will walk off. At least the course is there to play. That's just one man's opinion, and I do own clubs. It would most likely incur less damage than an ATV trail on the golf cart path.

By her third year, Bena was developing a reputation. If you wanted a pheasant—or at least a shot at one—hunt behind her. She put up with most people. I had socialized her in all the manners I could think of, but she wasn't a house dog—and she never pushed the issue. Since the wife was not an animal person, Bena lived in a nice winter-insulated and summer-shaded kennel. When she was out, it was time to work. She knew it and was all about the business.

If I have a weakness as a dog partner, it is that no matter how hard I try, I sometimes over handle the dog. I can't tell you why Bena was a close-working shorthair; she just was. I didn't have any electronics to remind her to stay in some reasonable zone to the hunter. For the most part, she just did. A whistle by mouth was about all I needed to keep her around.

Coming from a Lab background, where their job was to flush a bird, I always worked to keep them in range when they flushed. I even went through some withdrawals when she would range occasionally to fifty yards. Buddies I hunted with who had no feel for pointer work would absolutely go bonkers. It wouldn't be ten minutes into the hunt, and they would try to reel her in to twenty yards.

As time went on, I developed greater confidence about her abilities. I would encourage her to work farther out. She was trained to track, and sometimes on a running rooster, you just couldn't keep up with them. Two things were going to happen if we ran a rooster: She would catch up to the bird and set it on point, or it would flush long. Either way, in front of her, it wasn't going to end well for the bird. If we could get a long runner in the air and mark where it set down, it was as good as in the skillet featuring onions, gravy, and rice.

The following are some stories that I hope will help educate you about the breed of shorthair and what they can offer. More importantly, this is what I learned about other humans and myself.

COUNT TO THREE BY ONE HUNDREDS

If you've never hunted over a pointer, then this is good advice. As you hear the bird getting up from under your feet, start to count. One, one hundred, two, one hundred, three, one hundred. Then shoulder your gun. If you're the one kicking out the bird, it may be right under the dog's nose or a couple steps away. Regardless, it unstrings most folks, and they empty the gun before the bird is out far enough for the pattern of shot to spread and help them with accuracy. If they luck out and hit the bird, the table fare is usually a side dish of shot with what might be left of the bird.

I was hunting with a classmate from school. Bena had locked tight on a patch of grass on the edge of a cut field. I never want to be in front of the guy who is going to be shooting when I kick out the bird. In some cases, it makes me nervous when the dog is in front of them—even as close to the ground as they are. I had him at the ready, slowly walking behind Bena. Bena would only move forward if the bird moved. It was an attempt to set the bird again. On set birds, she was so solid that if you pushed on her, she'd fight to remain steady. When she stayed locked, I told him to walk around her and then start kicking the grass and remain ready.

He kicked at the grass like he was working to stomp a cockroach. Nothing moved. He looked at me and had about half a word out to say, "Nothing there."

Suddenly, the big old rooty (local slang for male pheasant) climbed up his back and headed south. The gun was emptied before the bird hit the thirty-foot mark, and it was a pump gun with a tight full-choke pattern, which didn't help his accuracy any. It was an awesome display of working the pump action nonetheless.

When he turned back around, his eyes were as big as saucers—and the color had all run out of his face. "Sorry," he said.

"Don't apologize to me. Tell her," I replied. "She's the one that got shortchanged for all her effort."

That only made him feel worse, but to be honest, I was grinning inside. I got to grin a lot behind that dog. I wouldn't let on that even I was on the learning curve with her. Sometimes she did things that required me to take considerable thought to eventually understand them. But one thing for sure was three words: Let her hunt! My job was to listen to the whispering.

Chapter 8

BELIEVING IN THE NOSE

I'VE BEEN LUCKY TO HAVE been positioned in life where I was exposed to, or got to know, an array of outdoorsmen and women. Some of it came from working sporting goods retail, and some of it came from being involved in conservation organizations and outdoor clubs. Later in my dog life, I was able to hunt and fish alongside some of the finest outdoor writers while I worked for the privately held brand Camp Chef. There will be more about them later—unless a couple of them encourage me to burn this writing.

I met Lloyd at an outdoor shoot for a local archery club. In the early 1980s, Utah had deer numbers and a liberal bag limit of two bucks for archery tackle. I cut my teeth learning to bow-hunt in Idaho, but I'd never met anyone who hunted with a bow and arrow from a tree stand or ground blinds. Mostly they did what was called "still hunting." It's a method where you move a little through the woods and pause and look a larger amount of the time than you move, hoping to spot the animal before they do you. Then you attempt to position yourself for an opportunity to take the animal. It's hard to do, and for the most part, you'd have a tag all season. That is why I guess it was called "still" hunting.

Fred Bear, the father of modern bow-hunting, said, "If you want to see game, move around. If you want to kill something, sit still!" Lloyd was a master of sitting still. He was the "natural cover" ground blind king, and he taught this roving hunter how to do it. We both enjoyed waterfowling and pheasant hunting, and we started chasing birds together as well.

I knew that wind direction was important to bring game to the bag, but nothing taught me more about the importance of wind than when I set a blind for bow-hunting—except hunting behind Bena. I'd taken a lot of that "wind and scent stuff" for granted as a young budding bird hunter with Dolly. Most likely, I didn't even give it any thought.

Genetically, some dogs may have noses better than others, but you can help bring a dog's nose into play during the training process and by how you set up your hunts in the field. Sometimes there is just too much scent or too many scents in an area, which confuses the dog. I think of it like dropping a couple handfuls of change on the table. You have a couple dollars in each hand of various coins. The confusion comes when someone tells you to pick up $2.36. Easy enough, you can see the coins. If they tell you close your eyes and hand them $1.18, maybe you get close or accomplish it by feel because you handle change from time to time. Now, let's see if you can sniff out a quarter and hand the same change.

Lloyd had a part Lab, part Shepherd cross that held his own pretty well as a hunting dog. Jake was getting older and had some physical issues coming with age. Since I had this new pheasant mower, we just took Bena. Neither of us were fans of opening days and the human antics that often went with it. On this particular opener, we opted to go later—after the mobs had left the fields. It was a snow day, and it took all I had to delay the time to depart. Oh, I loved to hunt roosters in the snow.

I had my eye on some barrow pits along a country road that I was pretty sure would be overlooked. There was a two-acre weed patch adjacent to the road with about fifty yards of sparse cover between them. The layout was such that most folks overlooked the road cover. They pushed birds from the patch as they hunted it toward the cover along the road. Or the birds would squirt south as the hunters walked west toward a natural canal that they used to block moving birds. The commotion of unloading hunters and dogs from trucks was usually from the north. It was always a mystery to me how they never spotted a pheasant moving south through the lawn height cover as they slinked out of harm's way. The birds would all run up and across the road, heading into the southern side cover along the opposite side of the road. So, for some time, they would be exposed to hunter sight.

I know some of you are thinking it may not be a safe place to hunt, and you'd be right because of an experience I had in another area along a road that I will cover later. And some of you question the legalities and maybe the way it looked to the nonhunting public. We never shot within the road right-of-way or across the road to remain legal. And you could see vehicles coming for at least half a mile in each direction. You would stop your progression if a vehicle came along. As far as how it looked? In those days, hunting was still an honored tradition and accepted by a majority of folks. Most people had a relative who hunted. I wouldn't hunt there nowadays if it was full of birds, and I was paid for each one. Most people wouldn't understand it, and it is likely that someone would stop and hassle me. Then I'd have to muster all my patience and spend hunting time explaining why I could. I just don't want to deal with that.

I'd park the truck to look like we were just walking back to it and not give the spot away to passing hunters. The large patch across the road to the north always got hunted too quickly by folks, and that was the strategy for the other spot to produce. On that day, folks were still there when we pulled up. Three guys with four Labs were just loading up to leave. I saw no tail feathers protruding from their game vests, and I figured we still had a chance.

I told Lloyd we'd hunt it when they left. I can't remember the exact conversation, but he had his doubts. I was pretty sure the birds were either hanging along the south edge or had boogied it across the open grass and over the road. We started on the edge of the large patch. The tracks leaving it were hard to see in the melting snow, but there was enough sign to believe the roadside would hold birds—and there wasn't a human track headed that way.

We circled the patch and then cut right through the middle of it, hunting the crosswind. We could pick up the other part of the patch if we needed to on the way back. Bena set the first bird, a single, twenty yards from where the hunters had loaded their dogs to leave. The second set was a pair. A rooster and a hen were held tight in the middle of the patch, and there were no tracks into where they had launched from. The birds had sat there all morning.

There was so much human and dog sign in the patch that even I was a bit impressed that anything was left. We walked to the head of the barrow, knowing that the birds would have to either travel up or down once they got to cover to get as far from the commotion as possible. That choice of direction was pretty much a coin toss, but it was somewhat dictated by the wind. In this case, we wanted to hunt into the wind to cover our walking noise because I was sure the birds were on edge from the pressure. We hugged the north side to help position the birds to the south edge to up the odds that they would launch away from the road so we could shoot. We were about forty yards from the end of cover, and we had spent the past fifty yards walking on top of pheasant tracks headed down. I didn't get a good count on the birds that came up and continued to come up while Bena was gathering up the final two of our daily bag, but it was several.

It may have been that experience that woke me to the true value of a shorthair's nose. The amount of commotion and scents that had been in the acreage patch was unbelievable. We had seen a couple of places where someone had taken a bird from the sign that was left in the snow. How she sorted through all that was just a mystery—and maybe it should always remain one.

I had taught Bena to track with a drag cloth. I would dip it in pheasant scent and then drag it along the ground with a seven-foot fishing rod so that the scent trail was outside of my tracks. It was short trails at first, and then I expanded the length and difficulty as she found success. Her reward was that she'd find her favorite bumper at the end of the trail soaked in scent. I knew where the bumper was, and after she had learned to whoa (stand still to bird sighting or scent) using a rod and wing on sight, we moved to whoa on just scent, using the bumper.

I had a guy tell me once that his dog got his limit for him. The deeper into the upland world I entrenched myself, the more I would learn that disheartening effort wasn't necessarily uncommon in these parts. The last thing I wanted was my dog catching birds! She only did it twice in all her time afield. The first time, it embarrassed me to no end. And I learned again to trust the nose.

Bena and I were hunting the Sunday of an opener in a popular hunting unit. It was fairly vacant of humans on that particular day. We were walking a canal bank. She kept drifting down to a patch of tulles that ran parallel to the canal with about twenty yards distance from us to the cover. The patch was too large for us to manage, and I kept bringing her back up and away from it.

All of a sudden, a couple hunters popped out onto the canal at the corner, some fifty yards ahead, and they started toward me.

I stopped and whistled at Bena because she had disappeared into the patch. She no-showed on the whistle—dang her! The hunters got to me, and we exchanged greetings. About then, there was some commotion from Bena in the tulles.

One hunter went on guard, and I told him it was just my dog down there. I whistled to her. Another no-show!

The one hunter said he'd been out on the opener and didn't shoot a bird because his other friend's dog did most of the killing. They asked me what breed my dog was, and I told them.

The hunter said, "Yeah, that is what my friend had."

I told him they could be trained to not do that—and that mine never had.

About then, I looked down toward the cover to see Bena coming out with a large rooster in her grasp! It was very much alive. Geez—of kids and dogs!

I took it from her and gently scolded her for making a liar out of me. So, here I stand with this pheasant and a couple hungry-to-get-one hunters. It was a catch-and-release kind of situation that was complex with the ethics of fair chase. Should I reduce it to my bag? It was my dog after all. Should I go hide it along the ditch and tell the hunters to go find it? Should I hide it and see if Bena would find it and then one of them could kick it up and shoot it? Or should we just toss it and let it fly away?

They were good with the tossing, but I could tell they didn't really want it to get away. So, it was kind of a jump-ball kind of thing. I heeled Bena and set the pheasant on the ground. I would no longer be a party to it. It just sat there.

They tried to get it to fly, but it wouldn't. Finally, with a little more foot prodding, it tried to fly. It just fluttered and flopped down off the canal toward the cover. I knew it wouldn't make it; most likely, Bena had hurt it while catching it. I sent her to retrieve it.

When she got it to me this time, I noticed blood on it, and that helped me discover the broken wing tip and a wound in the back. The bird had been shot the day before and had either taken cover or fallen in the patch. The wind had been such that Bena could smell the bird and the blood. Most likely, that was the reason she had kept drifting to the patch. Blood smell was the sign to get it gathered up to her, I reckon. She had restored some faith in her breed to the two hunters. The other bird? Oh, the bird? I almost forgot. One of the other hunters asked if he could have it.

Bena said that would be fine. She knows I'd rather shoot my own.

One other time, Bena went on point, directed at a patch of dried willows that were bent over like an igloo covered with snow. I kicked and bounced with one foot on the willows, trying to get what I hoped was a pheasant in the air. About the time I decided to pull her off, thinking maybe it was a mink or some such issue, she broke point and went under the cover. She emerged with a very wildly flapping "hen" pheasant. Blood was spraying everywhere.

Crap—another dilemma!

Bena had a soft mouth, and I didn't think she could have done that damage. Digging in under the willows, it looked like the pheasant had been sitting there for a while on top of a blood spot. Again, I think Bena smelled the blood and thought the bird was fair game to grab. Now, what to do with the illegal pheasant? Illegal? Yes, it was a hen—and you could only shoot roosters.

I didn't shoot it, but it was now in our/my possession. If I left it, I'd violate a "wanton waste of game statute." But it wasn't really game because it wasn't legal to pursue that sex. Even though I didn't shoot it, "we" now possessed it. Because of our partnership, it was a "we" thing. I could have told her to drop it the second I saw her with it and then walked away. I knew it was critically hurt, and wasting it wasn't on my list of acceptable practices.

I knew the warden, and I had even hunted birds with him, but it would be late before I could get to his house with it. It was before cell phones, so I couldn't call and even leave a message that I was coming his way with a bird that wasn't legal game. It was truly a catch-22. I decided it was Bena's bird because she had initiated it. How could they write her a citation anyway?

I decided to let God sort it out. Bena was really in trouble. Hunting without a license, illegal sex in possession, and a method of take violation.

When they tell you what kind of weapon you can use, a dog mouth isn't listed. There was only one thing to do: add a few more onions! Hens taste a lot like roosters, but I think they are not quite as mild as blue heron. (That's a joke, OK? Heron tastes fishy.)

What I liked about the posted hunting units is the amount of land one had at their disposal to hunt. Midweek afternoons were a good time to hunt. Some flood irrigation was still being done, and I could drive along a field on a county road and let Bena hunt. Birds would come to the edges of the gravel road to pick up gravel for their craws, and then they would walk off down the irrigation ditch to hold up for some of the day. She'd pick up a track and then off down the ditch she'd go. If she set a point, I'd get out of the truck, walk down the ditch, and put the bird in the air. It wasn't my preferred method of hunting. Mostly, I would do it to show off to someone on the list who wanted to hunt with her. I was truly into my snob mode by the time she was three. In her fourth spring, she had pups. I'll be right back to pups and my opinions of, and views on, breeding—after the story of her greatest nose challenge.

I was managing the sporting goods portion of a surplus store while I attended college. One of my customers became a good friend, and we spent falls guiding for deer and elk for a local outfitter. His parents owned a restaurant called the Juniper Inn. It was great food and was named after the Jardine juniper tree that is a hike to sight in Logan Canyon. It's an old, old, old tree. His brother still has the Juniper Take-Out in the middle of Logan with many of the old menu items. It has great food, and if you're ever in a position to eat there, it's just north through the first parking lot off Highway 89 as you turn off Main to head toward Logan Canyon. The original eatery was lost in a fire some years ago—and with it went a very large rooster pheasant mount.

My friend, we will call him Kelly Hoth because that is his name, had stopped in to purchase something, and I asked if they had gone hunting pheasants on opening day.

He said they had gotten a couple, but they lost a really big one that they only broke the wing on. They were just south of the Smithfield golf course, which now is gobbled up in housing. He said they thought it got into a ditch and ran. That was on Saturday. He was in the shop on Tuesday, and I convinced him that if it was wounded and hid up, then, most likely,

Bena could find it. He was on for the try because it had been such a large bird, and he had wanted it for a mount for the restaurant.

I could tell he had his doubts.

On Wednesday morning, we went to the ditch. I put Bena down it and told her to hunt. In about forty yards, she threw a point. I looked at Kelly.

He said, "Naw, no way." He carefully pulled the drooping grass back that was hanging down in the dry ditch to reveal a rooster tail. "It's alive," he said.

"Well, grab it," I said.

He pinned it to the ground and then picked it up. It didn't flinch.

I put Bena in the crate and helped Kelly into the front because he was two-handing the pheasant like a football. "How do I put this thing out humanly without hurting the feathers for the mount?" he asked.

My best guess was to choke it out (sorry to any nonhunters who might be reading this).

So, he did, and it went to sleep. He laid it on the dash, and we headed to his home. I remember getting choked out in high school, but I woke up—and so did the pheasant while I was driving 55 mph down the highway! I managed the vehicle, concentrating as best I could, as Kelly tried to capture the four-pound fly buzzing around in the cab! By the time I'd pulled over, he had captured it and put it to sleep for good. There were a few feathers floating around—and blood everywhere from the broken wing—but it truly was an amazing find!

Chapter 9

LET US TALK PUPPIES, SHALL WE?

I HAD SEVERAL HUNTERS WHO EXPRESSED interest in having a pup out of Bena. All I needed to do was find a worthy, "papered" male, and we'd be able to fulfill those requests. I found a good-looking, light-colored male that had plenty of birds under his belt and fair manners. The odd thing is that I have no recollection of his name, and time has removed the copies of papering I once had. Time has taught me that puppies are a lot of work! And if you make a mistake, and they contract parvo before you can get their shots, you are in for it! Thank goodness for a good vet.

I'd taken the puppies a short distance off my property when they were maybe six weeks old. It was all downhill from there with parvo. They spent a few days at the vet with IVs, and, luckily, all four pulled through. Two of them never contracted it for some reason.

The vet knew I felt bad enough and never sent insult to injury. She remained my vet for years after that incident. The vet bill negated any profit I might have seen from the sale of the pups. I wasn't in it for the money, and all the pups found good homes.

The boy across the street ended up with one of the darker-colored pups, which he named Heidi (go figure). She was the spitting image of her grandmother, and for twelve years, she kept this lad on the straight and narrow out in the fields, putting the hurt on the roosters. It was fun to be able to watch him build the dog. Genetics can give you coat colors and conformation (structure and size), and it can contribute to temperament, but what really builds a dog is the training, obedience, dry drills, and then birds in the field.

I mentioned coat color. I like a light-colored pointer because they are easier for me to see in the brush just as the writers had said. However, melting snow created issues because land and snow melting becomes camouflage patterns that looked a lot like Bena's hide. I walked past her more than once while she stood statue still in that environment. Today's GPS systems would have alleviated that issue.

I cannot get my head around all those electronics hanging off my bird dog. I was hunting with a friend who had a dog he'd geared up to resemble the flight panel of the F-15s he used to fly. He let her run because she was tracked by GPS. It would blip when she hit a point. For the most part, finding her wasn't an issue. In one draw we hunted, we spent considerable time. At the end of it, he showed me the screen—and it was all but black with the tracking lines of where she went. I can say with confidence that she covered the bulk of the cover there.

I admit it was interesting, but it just isn't yet for me or my dogs. However, there may be some merit for my aging long-line-running retrievers to be able to give them a vibration of when to give it up and return. You decide: would that be responsible partnering or overrunning the partner?

There are plenty of folks who make an honest living at breeding honest dog lines for all the good reasons. And there are people who shouldn't be allowed to even have a dog—much less breed for puppies. Over the years, my stance on pups has changed. I now feel like we should support reputable breeders and leave the creation of good dog lines to them. I feel this way for a couple reasons. 1) Breeders as of late are interviewing would-be owners for the benefit of both the dog and the new owner. 2) While price is always created by supply and demand, I believe the prices asked for some pups are crossing the border of insanity. If breeders didn't have to compete with the "hobby" breeder or "puppy mills," they wouldn't have to ask such high prices for puppies. Sure, initial costing to produce dogs goes up like everything else, but I believe that would stabilize if they didn't have to compete for market share. 3) You won't be out a hunting companion all or part of a season while she takes care of pups. Pregnancy can be hard on physical systems. I tried to explain to my wife how hard her pregnancies were on "my" systems. (Please watch for my book on marriage: *Other Strategies to Find Time Outdoors*. I'm kidding—but maybe not though?)

In the following chapters, I'll continue to relate the prices I paid—or didn't pay—for my dogs. This might give you some guidance on selecting a dog that works for your situation. The purchase price is just the initial investment and will be the least costly action you may take. I have found that having an older dog in the kennel and what I call a "replacement dog" or pup brings challenges during the training cycle for the younger dog. I also find that a young pup around the older dog can change the function of the older dog completely. I'll have a couple examples of those challenges later on. Two separate kennels can help curb some of the challenges, but if you want to have the dogs in the home or keep them in one kennel, I'll just say it now: I told you so!

I did keep one of Bena's pups, Casey, for a short period of time to take him through obedience and then dry runs so that he'd sight point. In this case, where it was an offspring, it may have worked out where the dogs knew each other from the beginning. Star and Dolly worked better together than other pairings of dogs I have had. I just couldn't really afford another dog at the time. Casey showed tons of promise, and the offering I took for him helped me break even on the vet bills. Well-started pups that you can demonstrate with raises the price. In the 1980s, in this market, five hundred dollars was unheard of for shorthair pups, and few kennels sold started dogs.

By now, you should have a feel for what you need to start doing before you get a pup. There are so many good trainers and good information about training on the market. Educate yourself before you take one home. Some of the most valuable advice I discovered in the Walther books was the power of early obedience to set a foundation for the dog. Sit, stay, come, and no! You can get to those oftentimes quicker than you can dig out the electronics or get the whistle to your mouth. Those four words can help you bypass all kinds of heartache. From skunks and porcupines to vehicles, you can help your pup that you want to remain safe. The following is a good example of why you should drill these commands into your pup.

A couple fiends and I had just finished up hunting a weedy depression and were approaching a gravel county road that bumped up against it. We were about thirty yards from the road. I was in the center with my friends on either side of me. I whistled for Bena to find me and heel up, but she had picked up on a runner and was tracking it. I saw her burning up the embankment about the time I noticed the car screaming toward us. I yelled, "No, sit!"

Her butt pinched gravel, and the car tire flew by her at about four feet. I should have done a couple things different there, but luckily—because of the commands—I had a chance to practice them again in the future. I never again walked toward or along a gravel road with her without her being leashed. She was geared to hunt, and only the leash could take her completely off that instinct.

I was pretty sure we were finished because we had walked out through that spot and were approaching the truck. She just went back to work on a scent that had showed up in there after we had passed through. A leash could have avoided what could have been a tragic outcome. As you can see, even snob hunters are capable of learning—but I have a ways to go.

Chapter 10

POINTING DOGS DON'T RETRIEVE OR SWIM

ET US EXPLORE THOSE TWO myths in the title of this chapter. While some guides and Joe hunters I have observed are content to let the pointer point, they bring along another breed to do the fetching. I didn't have that liberty. Bena was to be as versatile of a field dog as I could help muster. Some of the best pheasant hunting in my parts was around water, and human hunters shouldn't swim to get the bird back. I believe it is all about how you introduce a dog to what you want them to accomplish. It was going to be a bit of a challenge for me to teach Bena to find the bird and then not touch it. "After it flies and dies, you can touch it. I expect you to bring it back or fetch it back." I put the fun in it early in her life. I wanted her to want to do it. I made the mistake of not truly understanding "force fetching," and I just about screwed her up. It took a couple weeks of therapy with her hanging out at my folks' place for dad to fix what I almost ruined.

Swimming? I live in a climate that is pretty much three months for each of the seasons. I didn't expect her to sit for a couple hours at twenty-five degrees in a duck blind, climbing in and out of the water, but I did expect her to get that rooster that she dug out of the tulles and that I dumped in the water back to shore in thirty-two-degree weather. And if it happened to be a duck that flew by and became part of the bag, I wanted that back also. I introduced her to the fun of water early, and I introduced the retrieve portion in water early as well. It starts with a bit of wading on a warm day and just monkeying around in the water with no expectations. The following story will illustrate why versatility is important.

We were hunting a place I called the fingers. It was a series of narrow points with thick cover that extended out into a large pond. You'd work each finger slowly out, and there was enough ground that the birds could work through it. They would work to the ends and then try to hide. Rarely would they break early if you just eased along. Then you could position yourself on the dog's point. This would up the odds that the bird would flush and fly in a safe shooting direction. If they flew straight off the end of the points, you had to let them go because they flew toward a road and farmhouses. But if they went behind you or left or right? Dinner! These places often got overlooked. I tried to hunt them midday after the birds that flew in had settled in from the activity of morning feeding. We had just finished the middle point to the end. I was right at the water's edge when a car pulled off the road directly across the pond, and a couple hunters with springer spaniels got out. I thought we'd watch the show, and we just stood there.

The hunters encouraged the dogs down this step embankment toward the water. Actually, the cover did more to encourage them than the hunters did. There was good cover there, and the hunters could stand above it for a good view, on the edge of the road, while they watched the dogs working. This place was within a posted hunting unit, but the laws still applied to not shoot from, upon, or across a road maintained by a government entity. The road's shoulders were included in that law as a "from" part.

I knew birds often hung up there below the paved road. The dairy farm feed spills were easy picking for bird food. Some birds just walked down to the water, got a drink, and hunkered in there until it was time to eat again. The older birds usually jumped the pond and glided into the heavier cover of the fingers. While the slope between the road and water always held birds, the cover was just too close to the homes for me to want to hunt it. The posted hunting unit designations kind of fudged on the law, which stated that you needed to be outside of six hundred feet from a dwelling or place that held livestock in order to discharge a firearm unless you had the written permission of the owner of said structures—even if you had permission to hunt the property you were on.

In Utah, if you are within six hundred feet of homes or outbuildings that enclose livestock, you need written permission from whomever owns the structures or the legal operator of the livestock or structures before you can discharge a firearm. It was just accepted that the first two days of the hunt would be nuts—and some "looking the other way" would take place. Most landowners either hunted back then or had family that did. Because of that, everyone just kind of overlooked it and went anywhere within the hunt unit boundary. You could post your property out of the unit if you wanted, but it required signage and painting posts with x amount of paint to designate your property was off-limits, and most folks just let it ride. Oddly enough, there were few issues from a safety standpoint. There was always a bit of butting in line, but most hunters want to do it right and safe. There are always a few bad seeds or two in any public event. Easter egg hunts jump to mind.

The dogs flushed a bird, and it took a path to the right of us out and across the water. We were out of the line of fire, so they shot. The bird went down about forty yards from them and in the water sixty yards south of us. Neither dog wanted to fetch. The dogs watched it fall. They ran to the water's edge and looked out at it. After a few minutes of "exclamatory encouragement," one of the guys climbed down, picked up a dog, and tossed it toward the bird. When the dog surfaced, it swam to the bank long of the hunter and went up to the car. The second dog figured it out and followed its pal.

Finally, I yelled and asked if they would like me to send my dog to get it.

The un-trainer who had tossed the dog hollered, "Pointers don't swim!"

That did it! You can imagine what I wanted to say. We'd just do a little demo. Bena already had the mark and was becoming unhinged by the minute to go get it. We'd show them.

"Well, she might," I yelled back. "Let's try. Fe—"

She launched about six feet from a sitting position and hit plane at "tch." She swam with silky graceful speed. When she got the soggy mess and turned back, I gave her the over signal toward the other hunters. She turned off her line and swam to the opposite bank. We were really adding injury to insult now! She reached the shore and set it down to shake the water from her coat. I called to her to come. She looked at the guy making his way along the bank, then over at me, and then at the bird. That brought me a tense moment. I was thinking, *Don't screw it up now girl. This is for your breed!* When she bent to gather up the bird, I yelled, "Bena, leave it. Come! Come!"

Begrudgingly, she eased off the bank and swam over. Only one hunter said thanks and waved. The other water expert had climbed up to the car. Yeah, the snob was all over me that day!

Bena acted about half bummed out over the ordeal. Fresh scent helped her through it. The last fingered point produced a rooster. I let her carry it back to the truck to make up for the one that, in her mind, she had earned—and then was told to give away.

I love a lot of things about hunting pheasants, and it is hard to determine what I like most. It continually changes, and maybe that is the beauty of it. There is nothing like a good old "rooster rundown," especially if it is against an experienced bird that has a head start. It is that event where your partnership with your dog starts to resemble a hunting waltz—or a foxtrot!

Surprise in Your Eye

There is a little dilapidated old barn inside one of the pheasant units. It has about ten-by-sixty feet of heavy cover on one side of it. It is just off some heavy fence cover on the way to larger expanses. It sits in a very obvious place that is easy to hunt. These small places are often the most overlooked places to hunt, and they get hunted less than expected. A slight depression that usually holds moisture so it can't be farmed is full of eight-inch-tall tight grass. It runs from the barn out to the east between two short-cut grainfields. That depression to most folks is coverless. To us, it is the birds' escape route. When the hunter slams the door on his vehicle and yells at the dogs as they unload them, the birds slip low from the heavier cover where they are shaded up, and they sneak through the grass draw to get out of harm's way. The birds can put three hundred yards between them and the hunters before they leave their vehicles.

If a dog can't track—and most can't—it's a quick trip around the best cover and remaining scent and then back to the car or a hike to the larger expanses. I've never seen tracks headed east. When I ease up to the area and find fresh hunter tracks—within a day—I'll follow them north. I'll make a wide swing and enter the grass to the east about two hundred yards off the barn, and I'll let Bena run. She covers it fast and hard, and the surprise is what usually sets the birds in the low cover. If we have someone else with us, I'll drop them off with instructions to ease into the end where it plays out and wait quietly for us to do what we do. That decision is based on what the ground around the barn relays to us.

On this particular day, we'd been had—even with as quiet as we had tried to be. She tracked them east, nose to the ground, and she never looked up until she pointed a hundred yards east of the barn. When I caught up to her, she broke point and started tracking again. I was at a jog ten yards behind her when she hit the skids a second time.

The birds broke just as I passed her nose. One flew straight away, and the other circled south and then west, back toward the barn. They were long as they caught air—near thirty yards. And they were forty to forty-five by the time I got myself together and tapped the trigger. I dropped the straightaway. And while Bena was gathering that one up, I watched the other sail back toward the barn and land short off it. After putting away the first bird, I heeled Bena. We eased back quietly to the barn, using a bit of a loop to come in from a side direction to cut the cover against the barn in half.

I figured the bird would hold to the first available cover along the barn. When I was where I was pretty sure she was picking up fresh scent, I gave her the sit sign and snuck out and around the barn to the southwest end of the cover on the south side.

Bena could still see me, and I gave the hunt signal. She immediately started to track. She entered the heavy cover from the east. She was working hard by the movement of the cover, and I could tell the cat-and-mouse game was on as she worked toward me.

In about a minute, the rooster pheasant came hotfooting it out of the end of the cover and saw me standing there. It squatted and tried to hide. It was maybe five feet from me, and I could see the surprise in its eye. It looked left and then right, and then it jumped up and ran back into the cover.

In that moment, I had a slight pause toward "catch and release."

Bena emerged from the cover with a questioning look in her eye. It was like the look she gives me when I miss—but with less disgust. Three directional snorts at the ground, and she figured it out and headed back into the cover. I ran south, away from the barn, so I could see both ends.

The bird had had enough, and it broke from about the center, climbing straight up into the air to gain air and safety. My catch-and-release vision was replaced by pan gravy. The #6 chill from the little Savage Fox caused the flight to stop.

Bena emerged from cover with her trophy. I'm not sure, but I think she winked as she presented it to me.

Never Miss, But ...

You know you're forgiven when she jumps into the crate or cab the next morning with that stubby little tail all abuzz. Dogs have a way of looking at you when you screw up what should have been a sure thing. While it's a strong look, it should not detour your resolve to remain afield. After all, someone has to be the senior partner—and they can't drive. This next story is brutal. It's an ego buster for sure, and it still pains me to this day.

Just across the Idaho line, a small railroad trestle crossed a deep narrow wash. The wash had water in the bottom and ran adjacent to a cut grainfield. I'd driven by it several times, but on this day, I decided I would stop and give it a look. I was a tad late getting where I was headed anyway, and I had time to spend there.

Bena and I climbed the grade to the track. She crossed over just as I was topping the rails with my vision. As I came over the top, I could see the other side. She was ten yards below me and locked up hard.

The bird had been picking up gravel for his craw along the track grade, and we surprised him. It broke as I slid to a stop just behind Bena. Remember that count to three by one hundreds advice? Well, I didn't heed it. I missed—twice—as it flew straight away up the creek. It was a gimme! I'm sure I got "the look," but I was busy looking at where the bird had flown.

Remember when I said if we got one in the air and marked where it went, we'd most likely get it? Well, this was the doubt that was left in the "likely" portion of that statement. Five shots later, it finally decided to fly to Oregon.

Bena dug that bird out of that wash three more times.

I'm glad we finally got it chased out of Idaho. Really, the last shot was just for good measure to help it over the mountains and out of the valley. We didn't need any "super corn chickens" breeding into the Idaho populations we hunted. They were tough enough as they were. The last shot really couldn't be categorized as a miss; it was more like a salute to a worthy opponent. Yeah, I'm pretty sure I didn't level the gun and shot straight in the air as a salute! And I followed that up with a song—an "outdoor anthem," so to speak, that was meant for those types of situations.

After considerable consideration, I'm confident that the bird had been picking up some kind of chemical-covered items that spilled out of the train cars. We will never understand what that toxic residue was that helped develop some lead-repellent force field around the bird. By that late in the year, I was using three-inch five shot with an increased number of pellets. Normal pheasants couldn't withstand it. All the sight pictures looked good, and that bird should have died. It was another one of those mysteries of the outdoors. It is still so vivid to this day.

All the way to the truck, I explained to Bena that this bird must have picked up some Idaho grain off the train car that had been grown near the INEL Atomic Research Center up by Arco, Idaho. I was sure it passed through there from time to time.

She just gave me "the look," and I made the senior-partner decision to drive home.

Hunting with a Knucklehead

I tend to forget the names of dogs that were issues in the field. Oddly enough, I sometimes forget the other team member's name. In this instance, I remember them both. Out of respect, I will just leave them to wonder who I'm referring to if they stumble across a copy of this book.

This particular dog was purchased "built and ready to go" out of the box, and the purchaser spent way more than he should have for what he got.

Bena had a fair tolerance for many of the challenges I brought her way, but she didn't have any tolerance for this one particular male dog. And to be fair, he was a fine-looking animal. Part of the problem was that he was a *he*. Now, before all you male dog owners burn the book or send me crap online, let me say I suffer a bit from Duke. And, honestly, most dogs I've been around in the field that are "challenged" just happen to be male. I'm just not drawn to them and the issues that seem to come with them. If they work for you, great. Bob Barker had a solution if you are not winning, and it will take some of the starch out of 'em.

This dog could have been salvaged as to field sense, but the dog's biggest challenge was the other part of the "would-be" partnership. The other part of the team was too busy with college to help the dog finish. On this particular day afield, we were driving down back roads, and I was sending Bena down the ditches and back, hoping she could throw a visible point—and then we could see if this other dog would recognize it. Our desire was to see if he could be walked in and would honor a point. Mostly, it was an attempt to continue to sort out where the dog was in his head so that I could maybe offer a bit of advice and see if we could get them both on some kind of a training program.

He just wouldn't leave Bena alone and hunt. It drove her—and me—nuts in the field. It was a ditch with nothing but grass along it. About fifty yards down the ditch on the downwind side, Bena locked up about ten feet off the ditch in a short-cut hayfield facing the ditch. Perfect! We circled downwind of Bena so the other dog could get a "snoutfull" of scent. About ten feet from her, he acted like he was getting it. We took him off the leash, and it was now playtime for him. He ran into Bena, knocked her off point, and started to bug her. Bena reestablished the point, and he climbed all over her, pushing her off again. She growled and then lit into him! It was a short argument. He ended up back under our feet with the "WTH look" on his face. Bena eased back to the ditch, slid ten feet to the west, and reset the bird. Amazing! My friend did kill the bird, but his dog was too traumatized to attempt the retrieve. Our hunting together was a short-lived affair.

THE ETHICS OF IT ALL

The college buddy, who I had scared to death on his first Utah pheasant hunt on the church farm, continued to hunt with Bena and me when he could. He had moved to Salt Lake City, and getting afield together had been a bit of a challenge. On this particular opener, he and one of his friends had traveled to hunt with us. The numbers of hunters in a party, and the cover being worked, sometimes add a challenge to the difficulty of getting everyone in on the action. Since it was going to be an opener, all bets were kind of off anyway. You went with what you were handed. A good pointing dog can help with the challenges of groups getting people set up to shoot safely.

On this particular push, Bena came out of the cover at the end of a ditch and started tracking through some ten-inch-tall pasture grass. I was on the end. She came my way, and I followed her while waving for them to hurry up and follow us. I was confident that when she got to the cover across the field, the bird would either break—or she'd set him in the railroad right-of-way.

When Bena made the fence line cover, I saw her pop up on the track grade on this side of the rail and lay into a point. Since that spur never got used, she wasn't in any danger of a train coming along. In those days, you could hunt in a right-of-way. I was watching these guys stepping long to catch up to us, and I was hoping all the while that the bird wouldn't break. I really wanted them in on all the action because I always got plenty.

When I turned back to look at Bena, I see a guy jogging up the track toward her. I was about sixty yards off of Bena, fifty yards from the fence, and ten more to her. The guy was about forty yards from her and closing, and he was walking briskly along the track.

I yelled, "Hey, hold up," and I started walking.

He kept walking.

I was picking up speed. *Maybe he can't hear me, but he certainly sees the dog. Yup, he sees the dog.*

He walked down off the track in front of her, kicked out the rooster, and killed it!

My head was playing all the tunes at once, and I was trying to pick out a meaningful lyric, but it just wasn't happening!

Bena had gathered up the bird from the field and gave it to me as I reached the fence. The guy was just across the fence from me, maybe at eight feet.

My buddies slid up to the side and just behind me.

I kind of feel bad about what came next, as I've looked back at it over the years, but I was a young, hot-to-be pheasant snob. I was also a hunter education instructor, and the manual never really covered ethics very well. Pretty much safety focuses, so what the hell? I failed to connect the dots back then, and I blew up.

"What in the *%$$, %$@$%,&&%$, do you think you're doing?"

He answered, "Hunting pheasants."

The theme of the lecture was that you don't kick a bird off someone else's dog when you're not in their hunting party! And it would have been as easy as that and ended there. I could have said, "Nice shot."

He wasn't looking for a fight. He was a young guy, all alone, and maybe seventeen years old. He just didn't know.

So instead of taking a breath, the next rocket stage kicked in.

He sorted through it all and said, "Well, keep the bird, mister, if it means that much to you."

I was a good shortstop in my hardball days, and the rooster became part of the double play as I stepped on the bag at second and gathered to throw the runner out at first! The bird hit him square in the chest. "No, sir!" I yelled. "You take this %^#$^ thing home and eat every $@#%$ bite of it!" I called Bena to heel and walked off toward the truck. I barely noticed the two pale-faced statues as I passed them. I think I heard them gulp as I passed. They followed behind the dog, slumping a bit like Linus in the Peanuts cartoon.

I've often thought about that young man. I certainly didn't "take one for the team" that day. Who knows what was lost by my response in terms of effort toward our cause? Maybe he just didn't hunt anymore after that and quietly went out of the ranks. Maybe he uses it as a positive experience in his life and is really out there helping the cause. But what if it drove him the other way and in the aggressive direction to help take away all hunting?

There is nothing wrong with honesty. In fact, we could use a bit more of it in all aspects of life—particularly in the out-of-doors experience and all which that connects to. It is the delivery of the honesty that usually sets the tone for the outcome. It's got to start with you working to be the bigger person in all areas of conflict. No, it isn't easy. You will work at it all the time. Karma and goodwill have a funny way of paying one way or the other. Paying it forward just seems to work best—and my field note journals are now full of experiences to validate better actions.

Chapter 11
HARD DAY DECISION

I OPENED THE KENNEL DOOR, AND Bena followed. We walked out the back, down the neighbor's gravel drive, across the culvert, and into the cut hayfield. I hung to the west, followed the creek to a sunny spot, and sat down. She had stayed at heel the entire time. This was one of her practice areas, and she was usually good for a set. She should have been running quarters by now, but she never left me. She laid her head on my lap. I talked, and she listened; her big, brown, feather-seeking eyes rolled up toward mine on every pertinent pause. It was time to make a hard choice. We'd put up with each other for the past couple years cordially, but we were just not getting anywhere fast. We certainly couldn't see each other in our future.

We'd discussed it, and so far, it wasn't overly complicated. I didn't see a need to escalate it. The "professionals" had concurred. Maybe the kid on the train tracks had subconsciously taught me something that day. Someone needed to take the lead if nothing more than to be fair to us both. So, when she got home from visiting her parents, we sat down and made the decision.

The next week, I helped her move into an apartment. We split things down the middle and worked to move on into separate lives. I kept Bena. My parents took her some of the time because of how life began to move for me.

Eventually, Bena would come to live with me again. She would be part of a new "prebuilt" family that came with a couple boys. Mike was ten years old, and his brother, Vic, was eleven. (Yeah, I know. What was he thinkin'?) Again, there is another book full of them mentoring me. The boys would soon be old enough to hunt. I would've liked to help them experience it, but Bena and her age wouldn't allow her in the picture. Pheasant numbers were fast on the decline. I just couldn't see having another pointer with less for it to do.

Bena's last point and retrieve came on a cold, wet November day. She had about an hour of hunt left in her, and she did her best to lean into it with that classic slippery slide point she was famous for that told me 90 percent of the time the bird coming up would have color. I stepped in front of her nose. The bird hit and grabbed air! I worked to fight off the thought that this may be the last one we teamed up on.

The bird crawled skyward, and time stood still. I could see the twisted tail glowing with black bands as it started that classic late-season flight dip at fifteen yards, which is so responsible for folks overshooting late-season roosters. I started the count: One, one hundred, two, one hundred, three … bang! Yeah, I never could quite get the counting perfect.

The bird came apart and looked to have fallen dead. Bena cleared the ditch like she was in her fifth year and trotted to the mark. She scooped it up without issue a short thirty yards off. She worked for position to gather and jump the ditch on the way back. Her athleticism was spent in the hour we were out. She hit my side of the bank a bit short, and I grabbed her collar and pulled her to land. The bird still fit her mouth like a glove to a hand. She shook, never dropping the bird. Then she huffed and puffed around with it, displaying what youthfulness was left. Finally she laid it at my feet and looked at me. Those brown eyes with a bit of fog cast upon them said, "It's all good, pard," but I knew that was the end of it.

"Fetch up," I said as I turned to go.

She carried the bird to the truck about two steps ahead of me, still working to convince me that she wasn't finished. I could hear the call of "last dance" echoing through my soul accompanied by the swish-swish cadence of my rain pants. By the time we reached the truck, my cheeks were wet—and it had not rained for the past half an hour.

By spring, she was gone. She rests on her favorite seat cover, buried under my hay shed, and keeps watch over my favorite bird hat. She was fond of the twenty gauge's result to her efforts, so I placed a few of the spent shells in with her. There would be more great days and hard days. Hard days come by being part of the dog clan. They only share similarity in death—in that it never gets easier.

Chapter 12
FIGHTING OFF THE DOG

OGLESS. I NEVER WANTED TO be there, but then again, I never pictured myself divorced and then facing becoming part of an instant family. The responsibility scared me off for a period of time. Lora is a patient, wonderful person. A few months of hard knocks and bad choices on my part brought me around. Not to mention the nudge from a few plates of her fried chicken.

Lora and I had not been married long. I was working at a sporting goods store when a coworker told me he had some Lab pubs for sale. It would be a good starting point in helping slide the boys into hunting. We had a big, fenced yard. We talked about it, and there was lots of enthusiasm. Lora had a dog when she was growing up, so she "got it." What there was not was commitment from the boys. Frankly, the move to get another dog that soon was a bad call on my part. We just had too much going on to give the dog the time and attention it deserved. As soon as the fun wore off the pup, so did the boys' involvement. Feeding and scooping poop were just not part of the fun.

While I was trying to get my personal life together, Bena had spent the majority of her later years at my parents' house. They allowed her to vacation at mine for the hunting seasons. She got along fine with the pup, but the addition of family responsibility and the stress of blending into the family—with the waning of the pup interest—brought another hard decision. Someone else needed this yellow Lab pup, which was now about seven months old and showing promise for the field.

A minister who was living and working by campus took Tia for us. There were still open spaces there for a dog to stretch its legs. The dog and his son of four years became inseparable. The last conversation I had with him about Tia was so full of thanks that I knew we had made a good decision.

As a new family, we were in the process of finding a bigger home and got lucky on a seven-acre bargain of property in the county. A round pen for horse training was the first thing constructed—and then the loafing shed and a dog kennel. I'd had a lifelong desire of owning my own horse. I also needed to confront the equine fear that developed from bad horse-related experiences during my youth. Those experiences seemed to expand as I had got older. I'm not sure how many more episodes I could stand from friends' "good" horses. Most of the challenges occurred during elk-hunting season. In many ways, the horses were like "un-run" hunting dogs on the opening day of pheasant season. Kennel door or trailer door—either way, it was wide-open spaces for each. I was sitting on a thousand pounds of decision-making, and I wouldn't be part of the discussion for the most part. The property headed me toward a solution for those challenges (another book, maybe).

I continued to fight off the dog for now. Bena was in her last two years and had moved back in. The boys were reaching their teen years and really didn't show interest in a dog. Both boys learned to shoot. They worked for one of my buddies at the hunter education center, cleaning the facilities and pulling trap. Pheasant numbers were in the tank. I couldn't get my head around the steel-shot garbage on the market at that time enough to get me back into waterfowling.

The boys spent the most time on big game and archery. But somewhere in there, Mike got a Lab mix they named Taz. If dogs could compete in rock climbing, she could teach the skill. I had a six-foot chain-link kennel, and she could climb out of it. She would go straight up the fence and out! Eventually we solved that with a lid. Mike had gotten her from a friend, and while I tried to help get her on a training schedule with him, it just didn't work. So, Taz became a family dog minus the hunt.

Then I got a phone call. The pup was four months old and not socialized. It was free and needed a home. My friend had adopted its last kennel mate and knew I was fresh out of hunting dog. In the back of my mind, I thought maybe I'd make another run into what was left of the pheasants. After all, I'd finished up at the top of snob class. I knew English pointers were built to cover ground, but I miscalculated how much ground.

She went to class, but with all the distractions of a more complicated human life, class wasn't what she needed. And her lack of socialization early in her life wasn't helping. Her drive to hunt was crazy, and she got there so quick you couldn't turn her. I thought about using my horse to keep up with her—like some of the quail hunts I'd seen on *American Sportsman* in my youth—but fences were an issue.

While my mustangs were solid mountain horses, jumping barbwire was not something I could teach them. Chips preferred to hunt alone for pheasants. She was headed down the dog "Buck" path, and that was an issue. I just didn't have the skills to help her—and there were the pheasant numbers to get in front of her so we could maybe sort it out. I knew nothing of electronics, and in those days, it was fairly new technology. Lion and bear hunters had been using e-collars the most.

The usability of technology wasn't near what it has become today. I was ready to try anything. I borrowed a collar from a neighbor. It worked all right—Chips ran under the deck and lost all confidence about coming to me. There really wasn't any good guidance on them at the time. If there was, I wasn't listening or looking. So, we gave up on Chips in the pheasant field. She was a good family dog and got along well with Taz. She took to retrieving and the obedience instructions. She was a fancy-looking dame— all white with black markings in all the right places. The name "Chips" came easy. She reminded me of my favorite ice cream.

She was kenneled near the horses, and they seemed to get along when she was out and about. I was always watching her for fear of a kick and wouldn't let her get in their way and completely underfoot. My horses' feet had been worked to reduce kicking risk, but you should treat them like a gun and assume it is always loaded because, well, they are.

For some reason, I decided to take Chips up the canyon with me to hunt grouse. Honestly, I don't know what spurred the thought to take her. My horse mentor of my youth lived to get high up on the ridges on horseback and hunt blue grouse (Duskys). I'd been having fair success at it, but I got tired of the continual search for downed birds being spoiled by Dolly and then Bena to do the hard part.

It wasn't without concern when I first let her out from the porter. I didn't know if she'd bolt, and I'd never see her again or what. I was saddled to get a move on as soon as she hit the dirt. Chips stayed right with the horse as we went up the trail. She'd make little loops away, maybe thirty yards tops. I tied up by a draw of pines that I wanted to work.

We'd just left the horse when I heard a bird get up, and I could tell by the short flight and wing motion that it had flown up into a tree. It was early in the season. There would be more. *Crap. Where did Chips go?* I was looking, not wanting to whistle just yet, and I noticed her creeping along in the bottom of the draw like a cat about to pounce on a mouse.

The first bird broke up my way, and I shot it.

Chips started up the hill only to lock up on another walking bird.

I started her way, and it broke and died.

Chips brought it back and then found the first bird. I feel a twinge of guilt for the amount of grouse she was responsible for removing from the forest, particularly blue grouse. I'd ride till she pointed or flushed. Often, I'd hear a flush, ride toward it, and find her at the base of a tree—looking up on point. It was the craziest thing. Chips had found her calling, and that calmed my feather fetish for a bit. I live in a flyway for local waterfowl, and they just wouldn't let up on me. I was leaning on the fence and looking skyward way too much for October.

Yes, no, yes, no, yes? Did I really want to get back into waterfowling? Yes, yes, I did. The reports were that the steel shot was getting better. Our family had grown from the two sons that came with the spouse package. We now had a daughter (Josie/JP) and another son (Riley/Ri). I had been able to introduce both of the prefab sons to hunting and fishing, and the second in line, Mike had a short run at waterfowling—thanks to Spud and Dolly—before steel helped us out of it.

The older boys were busy with the distractions of their late teenage years. Our daughter and our caboose son were just hitting the age where they could hunt in Idaho under a new mentor program the state designed to engage nonresidents who were interested in hunting there more economically earlier in their lives. Watching and participating fully in hunting are really two different things. Idaho was a fifteen-minute drive to the north. The Idaho Fish and Game's new mentor program was a bargain that provided more time in the field. The program also helped me justify the nonresident license fees for myself.

But there was a problem—no water dog. Chips was just not conducive to start young hunters behind or around for that matter. She took way too much management. Grouse on horseback wasn't necessarily a place to start a young hunter. If I was going to waterfowl again, I needed to find another dog to add to the kennel. I was in a better place with locality and time to train one. I went through all the death throes and justification of why *not* to get another dog and just make due to see if the hunting, in some other fashion, stuck on the kids.

I kept playing the tune from justification records: "Lots of folks hunt birds without dogs, including duck hunters," but the lyrics just didn't make sense to me. I couldn't get the rhythm, notes, and words to line up. I started to keep an eye out for a pup. Chips had taught me I just wasn't a good enough trainer to help a dog with established issues. I was pretty sure I could work through a pup again. Lab prices were still affordable for the initial justification to the loan officer (my wife).

The ad said, "Lab Puppies—purebred—$50.00."

Lora called to let me know she saw an ad in the paper. (Thank you, fried chicken). I arrived at the house, and both parents were on-site. The male was a moose of a dog, maybe ninety-five pounds, and the female was sixty to sixty-five pounds. Both dogs had good conformation, temperament, and manners.

"Do you hunt the parents?" I asked.

"Nope!"

"What about papers?"

"We never registered the parents," they replied.

Papers didn't really matter to me anyway. They were just an added bonus. Dolly didn't have papers. She did fine. I watched them for a bit, and then I picked out a female that showed neutral enthusiasm. I'd be training two kids with guns and a new pup. I didn't want too much zeal from the pup.

The next step was the name. What is in a name? Everything! The kids finally settled on Cocoa. It was a Pepsi-Coke battle for a while; after all, she was a Chocolate Lab. The wife threw in the name *Her-She*—the spelling is correct—just for confusion, and she almost won. More fried chicken may have pushed it over the top! I leaned fairly heavy that way, but I really wanted the kids to solve it. I needed at least one to buy in.

Chapter 13

WINNING?

SOME DAYS, I WONDERED ABOUT this pooch. She certainly had her own way about things. But really, Coke (short for Cocoa, yeah, I know, how's your kids?) was coming along pretty well. Chips had adapted to the kennel mate, and since she was so challenged in the winters with the short coat, she welcomed the brown heat addition in the kennel house. Coke could take the cold. It would be twenty-two degrees out, and she'd run around and get hot until she had to cool down by lying in the sump pump ditch. Heat? Well, we had to watch her—and lots of breaks and water. She was happiest frozen over with a coat of ice.

I want to divert here a little and talk about a couple challenges to outfitting young hunters if you become one or are so inclined. It all relates to conservation. When I worked in sporting goods retail during the eighties, I was always frustrated by the shooting industry and its inability to build guns and compound bows that fit small-framed individuals. One manufacturer took a whack at it by chopping off the barrel and calling it a youth model. Swing and a miss! All that did was insult those who knew different. Really, it was the archery industry with the compound bow emergence that was the most aggressive at working to get a compound to fit small-framed shooters. Even with those efforts, I ended up "tricking" bows to fit the smaller shooter. It took a few years for the gun guys to figure out what a gun with a shorter length of pull (stock length and trigger reach when shouldered) would do to motivate the smaller and younger shooter. The Winchester Ranger was a great little gun. They shrunk the stock and the reach to the pump, and they shortened the barrel. Mossberg was right behind them with innovation, introducing the Bantam model. Mossberg has maybe the most customizable pump shotgun at this writing for small-framed shooters with the addition of the versa stock. The safety on top of the tang is very visible and easy in function for the operator as well.

I was a short-reach kid and still am as an adult by most measurable standards. I remember the frustrations I had getting that old .20-gauge Savage Fox up to my shoulder when I had on my duck coat. It was 14¼ pull, and I'd been better off at thirteen inches. Not having to reach for a pump slide to cycle a round was helpful for the long pull fit because I could place my support hand back farther under the gun where I didn't need to reach to pump the action. Cutting the stock off just never crossed my mind in my youth. I've always been in awe of side-by-side shotguns. That fascination was mostly brought to me by my father. The magic of his Winchester Model 24 just had me. Everything about it was cool. I don't remember any misses. Really, I don't. He used to say, "Autos and pumps are built for the ammo manufacturers." He also said, "If you can't kill 'em with two shots, you have no business shooting again. The bird will be too long."

There is also the safety message you send from being able to break open the gun. A broke-open gun will not fire, and it is easy for others to see that the action is open. If you fall in the mud or snow, you can see down the barrel from the back of the barrels and make sure it's clear. And if it isn't clear, it's easier to clear. You only have to keep track of two shots: bang, bang. Not bang, bang and a question: "Did I pump the third one in or not?" It's easy to load and unload. I just think it is less complicated for the new shooter.

I know there are many wing shooters who shoot well because they started on a single shot, but I like the ability of the second barrel to clean up a mistake when you might just wing the bird. In waterfowling, over water especially, it gives the ability to put a wounded duck to sleep with a quicker second barrel than a single shot, and that can aid in helping you get the bird to the bag with shorter swims for the dog.

I like side-by-sides with double triggers. I can't think through the selection of barrels integrated into the safety that many over- and under-barreled shotguns offer today. If the bird's getting a tad long for the improved cylinder barrel, I have to slide the safety left or right and then forward to pick up the modified tighter grouping barrel. That is too much for me to think about—much less a kid starting out handling a gun. I like to just reach back and grab the modified trigger for a tighter pattern of shot that many side-by-sides offer. My Savage Fox was a "single select." which means that the wider-choked barrel always went off before the tighter-choked one. I learned to live with it, but it wasn't nearly as versatile as Dad's double-trigger 24.

My older boys had suffered through an H&R single shot when they learned to shoot. That gun kicked like a mule, but the stock was easy to adjust with a saw. I added some lead sinkers into the forearm to tame the barrel leap. The Bantam youth pump gun by Mossberg had popped up on the store shelves as my other two kids became of age to shoot. We purchased one of those for the daughter, JP, for all the good reasons of fit. But the youngest son, Riley, wanted a side-by-side gun. It would have been cool to hand him down my Savage, but he would have faced the same challenges as I did while learning to shoot it. I had gotten around it, but I just couldn't see coaching him through it when there now were better-fit options on the market.

Steel shot had changed things with gun barrels. My Fox's barrels were designed for the use of lead only. Steel didn't conform to barrels already on the market like lead did, and you could damage your barrel by shooting steel through it. There were no side-by-sides available in a true youth model that provided the shorter length of pull stock and shorter barrel when we shopped for Ri's gun. The Stoeger Stage Coach gun was a short barrel with a long stock trigger pull. Cutting down the stock would have given us a true youth model that is now available. The .20-gauge barrel was only twenty-six inches long, and it was not overpowering like longer stock would be. He could put on a full-length stock as he grew. We opted for the Uplander model in .20-gauge for Ri and found a band saw. We cut the stock down, and then we slipped a recoil boot over the stock to come in at thirteen inches. When he got larger, we put a full-length stock on it as we had planned. He became a good shot quickly. I'd say, on certain days, he shoots better than I do—but I won't!

If a gun doesn't fit, the shooter has difficulty getting up over the gun and keeping their cheek down on the stock. Head up means a high shot. Add some clothing and a goofy shooting position like coming up out of a layout blind or twisting to get a lead on a bird in the field, and you are asking for frustration and a reduction of safety. I can't tell you how many Wingmaster pump owners I insulted when they wanted to pass the gun down to their kid and brought it into the store for the lookover. I recommended at least cutting down the stock since most kids struggled with the gun length. Even with that adjustment, the reach to the slide (pump action) was usually still too long for most youths to operate the gun safely and efficiently.

My double guns all have shorter pulls. Pumps and autoloaders still challenge my fit a bit. I've been able to get my Beneli Black Eagle length of pull down to 14¼ with the factory-provided recoil butt plate change out. It's still a tad long in some situations. My Winchester 3X, by fate of a screw anchor for the butt plate failing inside the stock, now sports a custom laminated wood stock 13½-inch length of pull. Thank you, Winchester Custom Gunsmithing. The waterfowl truly hate you. It's a magical gun!

Find clothing that fits—or get it tailored—and pay special attention to footwear. We no longer have to be members of the Lewis and Clark expedition. Those folks were tough. Most of us would have died on the trail. I can't imagine how they managed their feet because they walked a lot! Cold feet and sloppy-fitting shoes will not help the experience outdoors. It is a safety issue. A trip and fall could provide an unwanted ending.

What does this rant detour have to do with dogs? It is a safety issue, first and foremost, for every person and creature in and around the gun handler. It's a part of the responsibility that will keep the manufacturing machine moving that helps sustain wildlife through excise taxes. Specifically for the dog, it is safety from an unwanted gun discharge or misdirection of the barrel. When it comes to the dogs' job, dead birds just make their jobs easier and safer. A wounded duck in a current produces risks you may not have counted on. Easier retrieves are just better for the dog.

The Pittman-Robertson Act puts an excise tax on the sale of guns, ammo, and archery tackle. The tax is federal money that will be provided back to the states to support their wildlife agencies and specific programs. The state agencies are the keepers of our wildlife. There is a formula used to place the federal money generated by the tax. It is based off of how many hunting licenses are sold by the state agency and how many people live in the state. Even nonhunters and antihunters are counted and get to participate by just being here—everyone. Wildlife in America is part of the public trust doctrine. It belongs to the public. So, really, the wildlife and their habitats turn into everyone's responsibility. Hunter contributions by direct-dollar-item taxes are contributing the lion's share to help look out for wildlife. The formula is the easy math to help work toward the goal of "balanced, sustainable, and healthy wildlife populations." Deciding what that means is the challenge. The devil is always in the details. It becomes a matter of "value."

So, we, as a family, are winning. We have moved the needle forward. The kids are outfitted. We live in a place where they can shoot flying clay targets right on the property. They can get the gun handling down easier than most. They practiced a bunch. Opening day would be the Idaho dove hunt. My daughter wouldn't be accompanying us on this hunt. It isn't the typical dove hunt. It was a bit of a strategy mix. I'd see if I could get Ri in a position to drive a few pellets into a dove. The unknown that followed would be iffy: dove feathers in a dog's mouth! The jury was out on this one. If your dog can tolerate a mouthful of dove feathers, the other feathers are easy!

Chapter 14

HAVE A COKE

SHE WAS COKE IN THE field; it was an easy, sharp word, and when she heard it, she paid attention. Don't name the dog with more than two syllables. Leave long names on the paper if you have them. We drove up to the mouth of Bear Hollow, which was an old stomping ground from my youth. It was above the grainfields where the doves fed. There was water and brush for them to roost. If you were lucky in the Bear Lake Valley, you'd get a weekend to hunt them. Then the frost or storm would send the bulk south.

There were a few of the little gray rockets around, but we had not scouted them. We didn't have a pattern put together—or any real strategy but to watch some land somewhere and then try to get up on them while they were on the ground. We would jump-shoot them like mini sage chickens. The birds often used anthills to ingest sand to help digest food in their craws after they ate their fill of grain. They returned to the sage where the ant beds were abundant.

Coke was seven months old. I kept her leashed as we slipped up on the first bunch of doves that had settled in the tall sage patch. We were still back a tad farther than I'd have liked to have been when they took flight. They had just cleared the sage tops when Riley shot. A rain of feathers followed as a bird went back into the sage. Coke couldn't see for brush, but I was pretty sure she had eye in the direction of the commotion. I unsnapped the leash and sent her. It wasn't over a minute, and she was back with this mauled mob of feathers in her mouth. The good news was the bird was back, and she hadn't spit it out. She fought the feathers some, but she was too birded up to seem to care!

We set up later that evening on a spring and shot a few as they came back to the water. Coke had settled in a bit and calmed down. I wouldn't call the bag of birds photo worthy since she was still working to get used to feathers. Coke had a bit of a hard mouth and fought feathers a bit like she had a chew toy. Over time, she stopped the chewing and just gripped the bird well. She never dropped birds and made you ask nicely to "leave it" once she got them to you.

Bowhunting consumed our September, and before I knew it, the Utah Youth Waterfowl Hunt was on us. We were ready! The kids were shooting well at clays. Riley had shot a few feathered targets, and Coke was swimming for bumpers and had done some drills through the decoys on land. I had picked out a spot with ducks and made a portable blind. Coke had worked on the land with feathered bumpers. I had not gotten quite to the decoy water drills. I guess the hunt would be the beginning of that effort. I figured out a stake system to hold Coke steady while the kids shot. That way, I could make sure the kids were doing all the right things. Safety was of the utmost importance. Coke would be forced to watch, and then I'd turn her loose to see how she managed when the guns were empty. If a bird happened to fall, I had it all under control!

What is it they say about best-laid plans of mice and men? The blind was simple, but it was just a tad tight. There was plenty of room for Ri and JP to sit side by side. I was between them and behind them. I was close enough to grab either of them if barrel swings got wild. I drove a metal stake two feet in the ground because there were no bushes to tie Coke to. She was just inside the door of the blind, but she could watch yet stay partially concealed.

The season opened, and a flock of teal came settling in shortly. That is a hard duck to start out on. There is nothing slow about their movements. I said, "Now!" Both kids stood and commenced firing. I somehow lost my balance, went over backward, and collapsed the three-legged stool as I went! I counted five shots and thought I heard two "I got its." Good. They were empty, and it sounded like ducks hit the water. Perfect! I was trying to unscramble from the ground, stool, and blind when I heard a splash. The exuberant pup had pulled up the stake and was gone! She swam to the far bank and climbed out, finding a duck that had sailed over there. On the way back, she noticed the two dead ones in the decoys, but she couldn't figure out how to get them without dropping the one she had clamped in her jaws. So, she swam in with the one. It took me a minute to convince her that she could go back and get the other two. After the second one, the third one came easy.

Coke had drive. Later that year, Ri shot a duck that was an easy visual retrieve, and Coke just locked up and wouldn't go. She got to the water's edge and just stopped and looked at it. No coaxing would get her to go. Then, it dawned on me: the vest. I took off the newfangled vest, and away she went. I'd just put it on that day for the first time, and it bothered her. That taught me to train the vest ahead of field time in my drills. My dogs now can almost put them on themselves. Coke never used a vest after that. I now believe vests are tools. Sometimes you use them, and sometimes you don't.

It's really a pretty good lunch: Coke and a cold pheasant sandwich, and it was time we went to the field deli for the pheasant. My pheasant snob standing began slipping away with the passing of Bena. Chips put me up on the mountain, out of the crowded fields, where the elevation and lack of human sightings began to clear my head. The rhythm of a solid walking mountain horse aided my recovery. I had a Lab with versatile potential. I had a son who needed to be exposed to what was left of what I'd known as the Utah pheasant opener or the field circus. I acquired permission from a few landowners close to where we lived. Riley had heard the stories of years gone by. He asked if I was sure that we needed to go on that day. I was sure. I was a changed man, and I promised him I'd leave the ball glove up in the closet. Birds or not, it would be educational for him—and a test to see if I was truly cured.

We arrived at the first property and parked while the dawn was turning gray. Another vehicle was already there. Funny, I understood we'd be the only ones in on this place. Oh, well, let the education begin. The property fence posts and gate were covered up with orange paint to warrant off those without permission. I was sure I knew how that happened.

There was an individual in the local neighborhood who, under darkness, on the eve of the openers, took it upon himself to paint most of the area orange. It didn't matter if he owned the property or not. I was pretty sure he didn't have permission to paint all the areas he did. It wasn't a posted hunting unit, so it didn't fall under that group effort.

When I asked him what his activity was all about, he said, "Oh, it's to keep the town folk out so we locals can hunt."

No, it's that little slip of paper in my wallet with the landowner's signature that allows you to hunt a specific property. The paper does sort out any encroachment complications with other hunters when Cousin Joe shows up—and Uncle Bob forgot to tell him he'd given someone else permission as well. Getting written permission to hunt is just an awkward exercise. It's insulting to most landowners I've worked with, especially when you know the landowner and they know you. They hate signing anything. I'm referring to landowners who are connected to and still earning some type of a living from their land, and they cherish it. The discussion to get "written" permission usually ends with them giving some kind of a speech about their dislike of the Fish and Game Agency. I suffer from growing up in a different place and time where most landowners where we wanted to hunt or fish knew us, and we knew them. "Thanks, Joe. Would you want a couple fresh fish?" was about as complicated as it got.

This place had fallen under the self-appointed gamekeeper's spray can last night. I wasn't sure how the other group that was parked there would fit in, but it was pretty apparent they were going where we were. I didn't recognize the vehicle, but we would soon find out who owned it.

As we were stumbling around and getting ready to go, a man said, "Hey, is that you, Perk?"

My brother-in-law's brother-in-law, was parked there and waiting for the rest of his crew so they could go in on the same property. Everyone was related in a five-string banjo kind of way. Oddly enough, his nickname was Mutt.

After the genealogy lesson of how they were related to the landowner, Mutt disclosed that they had released thirty birds there the day before.

I felt a bit like Johnny-come-lately. It was a detail the landowner had left out when I got permission, and there was a chance he didn't know.

Another truck pulled up after Mutt's clan arrived. There were fourteen hunters, including us. We were closing in on the "ladies and gentlemen" announcement. I was pretty sure the last truck didn't have permission in any way, shape, or form.

I said, "When you're halfway down that grass field, we will come down and then go east and then down along the creek—if that works for you?"

Everyone in the family group was agreeable. The latecomers were dragging around and waiting for all of us to leave. I was holding the gate as the others passed through. Coke was no longer agreeable. Luckily, I had her leashed and was able to pull her off the annoying Chesapeake Bay retriever. She had had enough of that Chessy at the gate.

They had released the birds in a large grassy area down off the hill and in front of the gate, maybe ten or fifteen acres tops. They would push it down to the end and up against the river. The river there has high banks, and it's hard for dogs to navigate—not too safe in my mind. I never hunted duck on it for that reason. They only had the one dog. They started the march through the grass spread out about ten yards apart. We watched them work half of it with nothing getting up. I was pretty sure the noise they were making hollering back and forth was moving the birds way ahead of them.

We had walked slowly east toward the creek for maybe a hundred yards when all hell broke loose down by the river's edge. There was maybe forty yards of broken cover and sparse cottonwoods and blowdown between the grass and the river. It sounded like there was shooting across the river as well. *Lordy, glad I'm here and away from that!*

There was lots of shouting back and forth, and they had changed the name of their dog!

We shot a couple birds while we ambled along the creek, away from the commotion, and Coke was happy. I was happy, but Riley was still a bit saucer-eyed.

The gunfire calmed down within ten minutes. We poked around and eyed up potential duck blinds. We walked back the way we had come, leaving the lower reaches for them to hunt later that day. When we got back up to the trucks, the report was "zippo" for the push. No one on that side of the river had killed a bird. The folks across the river got to be a part of the planted push, but it didn't do so well either.

Ri just couldn't believe the commotion. I told him I had put up with it every opening day for eleven years when I was a pheasant snob. I did the math, and there were at least a dozen birds left around there somewhere. They kept us busy for the rest of the season while sprinkling in a few ducks for good measure. Crowded pheasant hunting is more often a game of chess under the big top. Check and checkmate are usually the result of patience and studying the other hunters' moves.

Chapter 15

COKE THE MENTOR

I SOMETIMES SUFFER A BIT FROM pointer trust. I'd let Coke get a bit long when she tracked and wouldn't hustle up into range. It was just leftover comfort and habit from hunting with Bena and the trust I had in her setting birds. I had to shift gears that Coke was a flusher. I would have to make some adjustments to the game plan with Coke. I have and have had excellent dogs with noses that I helped bring out using scents and training games, but I'm going on record saying that nothing can hold a candle to a good pointing dog's nose abilities to find birds. Getting the bird to set is left to training and, in the end, Mother Nature. It's the Mother Nature mystery that keeps it interesting. If we ever completely figure that part out, for me anyway, hunting will lose all of its appeal.

I certainly wouldn't call Coke a "finished" dog in the form of what competitive hunt trials refer to. I doubt that any of my dogs then, or now, would be considered "finished." They most likely would finish somewhere just below last place in one of those events. God bless those who play the game. Those events might give those of us who don't have the time, money, or whatever some drive and ideas to better our field experiences and maybe help lift our dogs' abilities a tad. I personally sum up my field desires this way: Find a bird, shoot the bird, and get the bird back with "good" dog work so it can be eaten as table fare. "Good" dog work lies in the eyes of the beholder. All the training and efforts sometimes just can't explain some oddball thing that you get to witness in the field. Some actions and reactions you just can't train into the dog—Pavlov and his dinner bell be damned!

The signal that I'd done all right with the fifty dollars spend on Coke came on a gorgeous November day in central Utah. The pheasant ranch was developed more like a farm than many put-and-take pheasant clubs. There was enough cover, space, and food that planted birds escaped and became part of the landscape. I was hunting with a friend and some of his direct clients that were also my accounts through him. I'd received word that a hunter who would be in attendance had a couple rock-and-roll ready-to-go high-dollar black Labs.

I debated about taking Coke. She was just two and change in field experience. Sometimes too many dogs are just that, and too many dogs and youth oftentimes add up to a mess. I didn't want to be that guy, but my friend encouraged me to take her. I did.

We split into two groups, and I was glad about that. I could make all the excuses needed for Coke's failures to a small audience. She did great, however. Somehow, both groups ended up in the same vicinity of some tough cover and a wide, long draw. A push was organized. The black dogs' names got changed several times during the focused event.

During a recovery in some of the toughest cover of several birds that were dropped, I heard the black Lab's owner say, "Guy's dog has another one." It rolled off his lips in a dripping tone with a disappointed drawl. At lunch, he asked me if I'd trained her myself.

I told him that my son and I had done the best we could.

He said, "I wished you'd done mine."

Neither of his dogs were sloppy by any means, but I think there was some competition between them that sometimes got in the way. I dared not ask what he'd spent to get them to the point they were. To divert the subject, I said, "Well, sometimes a duck dog has a hard time changing over to pheasants."

He agreed, and I thought we were done. Then he asked what I'd paid for her and "where she out of," which meant her paper lineup.

I really hated to answer, "Well, I just didn't get the papers on her," but that was the best I could manage.

"How much was she?"

I couldn't even pad it and say, "A few hundred." *This is going to hurt!* "Fifty bucks," I answered. I'm just not a good enough writer to describe his reaction. I really hope he didn't end up back at his breeder or trainer's place.

While Coke was part of the family, I encouraged Ri to take a much more focused roll in her care and training than I had been able to do with his brothers and their canine experience. Some of this activity roll was possibly due to where we lived and our station in life. She became a mentor to the responsibility of Riley taking care of something. Plus, having Coke with us in the field allowed Ri more opportunities than he would have had without a dog. It gave him an opportunity to use his judgment. There is no need to shoot something you can't get back. If the canal was too deep to wade in and retrieve the ducks, you could still shoot because Coke could get them. If the brush was too thick where the bird fell, Coke would dig it up. And there were times when you wouldn't shoot because of the risk to the dog's abilities to recover the bird.

The value to me was that if the supposed-to-be-human mentor (me) screwed up, then Coke would fix it. I put Riley's first wild rooster in his game vest before I'd put it completely to sleep—only to have it jump out and run for the tulles. I stood there with my mouth open and looked up in a panic about finding this alive-and-seemingly-well first bird in the thick cover! Then I remembered we had Coke with us. I'd been suffering a bit from being dogless in the pheasant field as of late. Duh! She was sitting there and looking at me with this questioning look on her face.

"Fetch up," I said.

In twenty seconds, she had cleaned the pie off my face.

Coke would continue to help fix me and mentor Riley. I recall a day in Ri's midteens. It went something like this. Riley took Coke, now later in her years, to a place we call "below the house." We hunted it a bunch, and the dog knew the place. On the way in, Riley jumped a big drake mallard and put it back in the water with a wad of better steel. The creek has a bottom in some places, and in other places, I'm not so sure. You want to explore those places with friend during warm summer days—and bring a rope.

As he tells it, Coke balked and wouldn't go to the bird. She would start out and then come back. This was totally uncharacteristic of her. That alone maybe should have told him something. She usually hit them so hard on a retrieve that she removed feathers. After several failed attempts to send her, and I'm sure some name-changing, he decided to just wade out and get the duck. It was a mucky bottom with little water. The last step before grabbing the duck sent him into the muck to his crotch. Luckily, he had his gun slung over his shoulder and was able to use it to pry himself out and get back to land. It took several uneasy minutes. Coke sat and watched. I have often wondered if she would have "done a Lassie" and run the mile to home and taken me back to help pry him out. Maybe she just knew she'd get stuck and was hoping he'd just give up and count it as a loss. Who knows? Aw, the mystery of Ma Nature!

It was approaching that hard time again. Coke was getting on and maybe had three years left. It would take a year to bring a pup along—and then she would have two left in the field, tops. We started the search. Coke and I had been guiding at the ranch, and I had a paper trail of dogs to follow up on for pups. I liked the black Lab that the caretaker at the ranch had. He had gotten the dog from a guy he knew in Idaho Falls. I called him, but he only had a couple yellows left—and they were male. I wanted a female. And I wanted black for reasons I couldn't even reason. He did say he had another batch on the way. I told him I'd wait, but I kept looking.

Some time went by, and I found out that the pup supplier had "double batched." By that, I mean someone hadn't latched the kennel doors. That was the "other" batch that got here shortly after I had spoken with him the first time. The second batch had three males and two females left by the time I contacted him again. We were headed up that way, and I told the guy I'd stop to look at them. They were in the garage, loose, and what a mess that was. It was pretty obvious they were running out of puppy patience. One little female, the runt, crawled out from under the wooden steps leading into the house, and immediately took to my wife, Lora. *Half the battle*, I thought. I liked the manners, attitude, and tone of his voice when he called her the runt. What I didn't like was the price tag. "Runt" opened the bargaining door. Dolly was a runt.

At the time, I was in sales and knew that all things are negotiable. Desperation sets in when your market is oversold, demand dies, and inventory numbers are high and need reduction. He had high inventory with the five pups left at that time of year. He'd crashed his market by dumping thirteen pups into it recently. I'd checked the lineage, and it really wasn't anything that special. Sound hips were a must, and they seemed to have that. While seven hundred dollars was most likely a fair price in his mind, it was overpriced to me. I didn't flinch when he told me the price. He'd forgotten that he'd quoted me four hundred on a yellow female a few months prior. I explained that I'd never spent more than eighty dollars on a dog—papered or not. I mentioned that there were still a few pups back in Utah to be had for a hundred, but we would consider the dog and let him know what we would be willing to pay to take her off his hands—if she was still available, and we wanted her. We made arrangements to stop back in and see the pup on the way back to Utah.

Things played out well in our journey. We could justify the responsibility of another dog. We had discussed it for months. I called the guy and said we would have another look at the bunch on the way home if he was going to be around. He still had all five pups when we arrived. He told us a male sale had just backed out, and if we wanted, we could include that pup back in the choices. Oops—he shouldn't have disclosed that. Then he hit us with the urgency statement that someone else was interested in the runt.

Right! I wrote the book on urgency selling. I hemmed and hawed and showed a bit of concern about her size. Then I told him I wasn't a fan of male dogs. He immediately took the price to four hundred dollars—if I wanted the runt—because he didn't think the other people were that serious about the runt. What? Oops again—and we were on the move to an agreement.

I said, "Look, I'll make this easy on you, I have two hundred in cash on me right now. You know she will be the last to go of the five here—if she goes at all. You'll be two hundred ahead and break even on the numbers you were at yesterday since the other folks backed out. Or I can go give a hundred of it to someone in Utah and buy a couple extra bags of dog food."

He sighed, and then in five seconds, he said "OK, I'll take the two hundred."

I wasn't trying to be a jerk; it was just a buyer's market.

The little black worm wiggled on my lap for almost a hundred miles before she settled down and took a snooze. We discussed names for most of the journey, and before we hit the line, we had it: Hope. Her papered name was Firestorm's Hoping for Feathers. And she would get feathers—more than I ever could have imagined. Hope was in her DNA. I hoped that Coke would accept her role as mentor. When we'd start training, I'd hope it would go well. When we'd start the hunt, I'd hope we could find her some birds. I'd hope there would be opportunities to guide at the ranch. I hoped I could teach her to run long lines. But what we all hoped for the most was that Mom would be able to get somewhat better. The doctor that weekend had given us hope. That was the reason we had traveled northward; the dog just happened to be along the way and about three minutes off the interstate.

My mother loved sage chickens as much as life itself. She continued to take me hunting as she and my father were changing roles after his accident. She made sure I had as many *other* life experiences as a kid could tolerate—whether I liked them or not (see piano and dance lessons for validation). Every time I got to the vehicle, she said, "Is that gun unloaded?" She showed frustration over my drawn-out college effort and couldn't seem to understand why I'd knock off in the falls to guide and hunt. After thirty years of not touching a fly rod, on her eightieth birthday, she took mine, built a loop, shot the fly across the stream, and pulled an eighteen-inch brown out from under the bank. All the while, she was asking why we just couldn't sink a bullhead under there because she was sure there was a bigger fish that wanted one back farther under the grass.

The woman could run a chainsaw and stack wood better than most men, but she was now in a hospital bed, unconscious with encephalitis. The doctor had told us that a cold sore had inverted itself and somehow was affecting part of her brain. There was a chance that she would pull through, but might never be back to her old self.

I only hoped she would be able to bounce back enough to continue to enjoy the grandkids she loved to spoil and see what she could help me make out of this pup. My mother had learned great appreciation for our dogs over the years. She needed to see and love this one—and learn why she was named Hope.

Chapter 16
MIXING MUTTS AND MESSAGES

’M CONFIDENT THERE WAS PAIN in raising Star with Dolly together, but I had forgotten it by the time I brought Coke and Hope together. With Dolly and Star, the age distance wasn't as big as it was with Coke and Hope. Dolly and Star were mother and daughter, and there was an established pecking order between them. Coke and Hope's relationship was a different deal altogether.

We introduced them as soon as we were home. Hope got the "sniff the newcomer" treatment from Coke and then the walk-off attitude. Her posture said, "Not in my kennel!"

Of course, Coke looked a lot like Mom to Hope. The nuisance factor was there. Coke went back in the kennel, and Hope went into the house for a month of socializing and house manner work. It started in the form of the "box." The pet porter was to be one of her "places." The socializing was the easy part with grandchildren around. Maggie—our lion-sized (in her mind) Chihuahua-Schnauzer-terrier/something or other dog/grandkid food-drop vacuum/doorbell/all-around clown—would take care of the other territorial and manners education for Hope indoors. It took about an hour for Hope to decide that lying with the kennel door open, so she could be half out and half in, was better than it being closed because she broke the complete barrier. It took about two seconds for Maggie to teach Hope food dish understanding. Maybe she did have lion in her after all.

Hope couldn't figure out why Maggie pretty much had the run of the place, and she was subject to conditions: no pup on the couch, no pup on the lap until asked. I'm boxed, and she roams when you leave.

At three months, Hope had the inside manners pretty much down, and we started to integrate her into the kennel. I wanted them together but separate until Coke got used to sharing some territory. I built a frame of chicken wire with a door to split the kennel. That lasted overnight, but I rebuilt it. That lasted half a day. Hope was the destroyer. I gave up and held my breath that Coke wouldn't hurt her in some way. Coke did let Hope know what was and wasn't appropriate, and that pretty much established the order of things from there on out. It took maybe two weeks for them to settle into a relationship. Coke seemed to almost like—at least most of the time—being a pillow.

I would run Coke through training and keep Hope kenneled to watch. Then I'd put Coke up and bring Hope out. Sit, stay, and come were established before she left the house, and we would run those guidelines continually with everything we did. The retrieve part was started also while Hope was in the house by using a small stuffed sock. It wasn't left for her to destroy. It was a part of "fun time," and when we were done, it was taken away. That was also a bit of a confusion point for Hope because Maggie had this stuffed monkey that she could just take it out on whenever she felt like it. She would shake it like she was killing a rat and then race around the house with it. Hope doesn't know what a safety release valve that monkey was for Maggie because all of that could have been released on Hope.

Hope was coming along in her learning, and everyone was getting along. I had Hope pretty deep into the field work by the time she was four months, including live birds and a gun. This dog was coming fast—real fast. Maybe it was just that I had more knowledge as a trainer. Maybe it was the four-legged mentors. Maybe it was her pedigree. Most likely, it was some of all of it.

Late in her first summer, I noticed something special about her. Riley and I were putting together the boat blind. We had cut and bundled some tulles. We were now zip-tying the bundles on to the blind that was in place atop the boat. I don't know why the individual bundles were not close to the boat while we worked. We had been tying them in bundles out of the back of the truck, and it was parked a little ways off from the boat, maybe fifty feet. When Hope started bringing the bundles to the boat without any encouragement—other than we were doing it—we knew she was a thinker. Life was about to get really interesting!

At her eight-month mark, I was asked to help with a large group of pheasant hunters at the ranch. I have never been a fan of group hunting. Two guns is fine to watch and keep track of. The degree of difficulty goes up as you add hunters to the pile. Pointing dogs that will hold birds in place give you a better opportunity to manage all the issues that come with a bird rising into the air among the guns and the safety lanes that are available to shoot in. Flushing dogs become a bit more difficult when trying to manage a bird into the air so that it becomes a safe target. Coke and I have worked together long enough that I can tell you when she is birdy, and then I can position the hunters into a safe advantaged situation for a shot for the most part. It is important that you lay down the rules as a "guide." You must lay them down with seriousness. There is no bird to be shot at that is as important as every person and dog having a safe hunt!

One of the guides was having some issues, and I ended up picking up another gun in my group. Five guns to watch would be awkward. I also didn't know how Hope would function in the commotion. She had worked a couple times with two guns, but this could be a little bit outside of her limits. It would be only the second time that Coke and Hope had worked together in the field. The first time went well, but it was a very controlled environment. So, with all those concerns in mind, it was time to get the group's attention about safety.

My speech goes like this: "Welcome, you are on a great piece of property with historic value to this valley. Please work to keep it clean by picking up any spent shells you may see on the ground. Today, you will be hunting with Cocoa and Hope. Their responsibility is to put birds in the air for you to shoot and then bring the birds back to *my* hand. They both like a good praise and a pat, but while we are in the field, let me control the dogs for your best benefit.

"Safety is paramount for all of us and the dogs. I will be directing you as well as the dogs to position yourselves for safe shooting. You are to shoot only at birds that come up and travel out in your lanes. No cross-shooting over into other lanes. No shooting at low-flying birds. We should be able to follow them up for another chance. In the event that you do shoot at a low bird and hit one of my dogs, please do it with one of the first shots, so you have another shot available in your gun."

I pause there, and someone always asks why. I always tell them they will need it when I come for them! That usually brings a halfhearted chuckle. I know the wheels are turning in their heads, and then I tell them the hours and dollars I have in the dogs helping them have a good time. I've never even had a close call.

On this day, the group had a personality I could mess with. I told them that we were the substitutes on behalf of another ranch guide and dogs, which was true to some point, and that both dogs were designed to be waterfowl dogs. We'd see how it went on upland. I told them I'd watched enough video on TV to think we could get through this and maybe get some shooting. I could see an instantaneous drop in the excitement factor on their faces. I lined the hunters out along a grassy side hill: one gun on top, three in the middle, and one on the bottom. I stayed behind a middle shooter just off their shoulder. This allows a hunter to turn and shoot if a bird slips out the back on a flush—without me in the way.

I sent the dogs, and we started. About twenty yards into it, Coke got busy and busted a nice straightaway shot. The guy just out of center dropped it. Of course, that brought out the bantering that comes with that kind of an event.

I said, "Watch that black dog."

A bird got up right under the feet of the shooter on top. He unloaded the gun on the bird as it beat its wings to get out of Dodge.

Hope watched it go, and I thought I saw it falter just as it cleared the end of the grass and cut around the hill. I yelled, "Back."

Hope took off.

Coke handed me the first bird, and I sat her to wait and see what Hope drummed up. I was a bit nervous that she would get onto some other birds and blow them out. I was pretty sure she had a mark on a downed bird. I see her tail disappear around the corner of the hill. In thirty seconds, I saw her coming back with the bird.

I have intended this to be a book that the whole family can enjoy, and I've worked to leave out the colorful language and use some other symbols instead.

One of the hunters blurted out, "Duck dogs, my #@&&!"

"Just lucky," I replied as I adjusted the Velcro fit of my orange hat.

It turned out to be a way better day than it could have been. I noticed a change in Coke. Yes, she was on in years, in her tenth, but she seemed to be content to dig up a bird and put it in the air. If it was a pickup of more than thirty yards, she'd just watch and let Hope get it.

This working relationship would carry on until Coke finally gave out in her thirteenth year. A miserable day that was—as they all are. She literally fell apart overnight. I had to catch a plane to a show, but my vet was able to see me immediately that morning. Riley had to lay her to rest by himself. That most likely wasn't pretty either.

She has retired to watching the boat and making sure it is at ready. The hitch sits over her most of the summer. Following are a couple of short stories about Coke and Hope working together. When dogs do that in the field, it is a thing of beauty. As far as I'm concerned, you need to make sure it gets finished off. You are responsible to not miss. Nothing is more painful than that questioning look from your dog! When two dogs give you the look, you almost need to seek counseling.

ONE

I've been lucky enough during the past thirty years to be able to walk into hunting from my home. On one particular fall day, I'd decided to take a little walk to see out back. The northern birds should be starting down in the migration, and oftentimes I could tell that by what the birds were loafing and doing on the creek. There was a big group of northern get-up, and I dumped two and then got greedy and pushed the shot length a tad on the last shot. That bird sailed into a pond. I wasn't a fan of that place because it had wire fencing in it, and while I had permission to hunt it, I didn't because of the wire. I liked hunting off it and getting birds on the swing. That was entertaining, and the dogs liked the dry land retrieves when it was bitter cold.

After getting the two birds gathered up, we walked toward the one I'd marked. As I approached a creek outlet, the bird got up and flew low across the water, through the wire, and to the opposite bank. I held my shot and told the dogs no! I was pretty sure he was now held up under the bank. If we could get him to come out, I'd have to shoot quickly before he made the wire, which means the shot would have to be taken in under fifteen yards.

Both dogs were at heel. When I got to where I last saw the bird, the bank was about two feet above the water with an abrupt slope to the water's edge where the grass overhung. It wasn't a good place for me to try to navigate, and it wouldn't be easy for the dogs. There wasn't a lot of cover, so I was sure the bird was back under the bank.

Hope was kind of clueless and was just looking around, but the old chocolate dog was on the hunt. She eased down the bank to the water's edge with her nose to the ground. She stood in place for a few seconds, tipped her head left and then right, and listened. Like a fox chasing field mice, she reared up on her back feet and bounced her front legs onto the bank's edge. The drake exploded from under the bank! Coke got her front legs wet to the elbows as her teeth sunk into the duck's butt! It was lightning fast. I was actually stunned! I let her parade around with it and puff like she did when she showed off. She seemed to be telling Hope, "Look, junior. This is how that is done!" It was amazing!

TWO

Riley and I had been helping a farmer with antlerless deer depredation control on his property. The property was within one of the last pheasant units left operating in the valley. We were offered a couple of permits for bird hunting. We had also tried to help the landowner's sons become more involved in hunting. This opener wouldn't allow them to come along, and it was just Ri, the dogs, and me in attendance.

It can get crowded for the opener. It is amazing how many long-lost relatives show up. Most likely, you will still navigate a human or two. We did get cut off by another hunter who got in front of us as we worked the side hill above the agriculture. He saw us coming and sped across in front of us and invited himself to be our blocker. Grrr! I worked hard to keep the old snob in the box. He killed one bird, which cracked the lid, and he missed another as he cut maybe a hundred yards ahead of us. He could see us coming along the natural flow of the hill, and he hustled to make sure he got in ahead of us. While I wasn't really happy about it, the "heat" I used to have over that kind of stuff had siphoned off over the years. I found that patience somewhere would have a reward—and karma would usually kick the other party's butt!

Coke's aged, methodical approach produced one pheasant in front of me prior to the other hunter showing up. It blew from the grass edge and worked to descend the forty-five-degree slope in hopes of ducking the pellets. Pheasants are notorious for what I call "the jump and dive." It leaves most folks shooting over the top of them. As this bird tumbled to a stop at the edge of the lower field, Coke just gave me that aged look. I called in the new marine, and Coke was content to let her pack it up the hill to us.

Hope did her best in front of Riley, but she never could turn a bird. I was pretty confident that the bark of my double gun sent them forward into the path the hunter had crossed ahead of us. I'd been keeping my eye on a place north of us and above where we had parked the truck along a main dirt road. No one had gotten in there yet. I think the truck helped keep folks off it. We swung down to the truck for a snack, water, and a new plan. The area above the truck was sagebrush with a deep wash through it.

The sage bordered a CRP field on top along the sage, and the CRP cornered into a cut grainfield. We slowly worked north up through the sage to the CRP. From the dogs' actions, I was sure we were moving birds. At the CRP, we turned straight east and left a hundred yards of the CRP that cornered the grain alone—on purpose. We hunted along a water check bump for two hundred yards and then turned north up through the CRP to where it edged the cut grain that ran east and west.

That edge had the tallest cover, and Riley walked that. I stayed down to his left as we headed back west toward the corner of the CPR. Hopefully, the bumped birds held there. About fifty yards along, the dogs got birdy, and a rooster broke behind and below me. He didn't make it very far. I was limited out, so I unloaded my gun—a move I would come to regret.

The dogs were on high alert.

I told Riley his job was to stay with the dogs at all costs. I was sure the birds had been resting and that there were not enough disturbances to push them running across an open-cut grainfield. The earlier walk up through the sage was most likely piling some birds into the corner. I told Riley to make sure of his target and that the roosters were clear of hens. I expected maybe half a dozen or so to get up.

The dogs were now all abuzz. Tails were spinning, and noses were pulling in the particles of bird dander as they tracked. They were hot, and

I didn't want to make any more noise than we had to rein them in. It was about to unwind! Never quit on cover, and always work it to the end.

The dogs were tracking hard, and Riley was ten yards off the actual corner when it all turned loose. I could tell that he was in that "ain't going to happen attitude" when she blew! Somehow, out of the mess of feathers launching in all directions, he pulled off a fine double of roosters. There was bird going every which way. I was watching in awe of how many sharptail grouse got in the air alongside the pheasants when the two dozen or so Hungarian partridges attacked me and my "empty" gun that rested open over my shoulder. Yes, partridge season was still on—oops!

Positive karma on pheasants though. Gotta love it! I give the credit for that day to my learned abilities to finally overlook more of the rude posturing by others in the field. Maybe it was just my age—or that I was just flat out of trying to convince others to have better manners while hunting.

The safety focus of hunter education cannot be argued. If you are dead, everything else is meaningless. For what remains of our hunting heritage, I'd hope that states would start focusing on field behavior slightly past the importance of gun-handling safety. In some ways, I give the effort little hope because of our electronic appetite to "just get over and through it." Do it all online! That effort in my mind flies in the face of what the hunter education program should be about at its core: teaching responsibilities of self, others, the wildlife you pursue, and the lands they call habitat. You can't properly fit a gun to a student over the internet. If the gun doesn't fit, then there is a safety concern.

If you're a legislator—or anybody else working to water down a hunter education program for convenience's sake—shame on you! Please take up ping-pong and stay at home. It's your home, and you can make up rules that benefit just you and yours there.

Chapter 17

THE BLACK CLUB

As I start into this writing this morning, Hope is staring her tenth year in the face. She has been a special kind of something in our lives. I will never know her full potential because I'm just not that good of a trainer. As a family and for what we do, she has been more than enjoyable!

There are three other dogs and their human partners that I have to give credit to for specifically influencing my joy with Hope. A local waterfowler, Kevin Booth, participated in an outdoor education expo here in the valley with his dog Hopps. His kennel name was Cedar Hills High-Flyer. He was an amazing black Lab that hunted into his sixteenth year. I was super busy with the expo, but I broke away long enough to watch Kevin and Hopps work on long retrieves during the demonstrations. I'd never built that into any of my dogs, quite like they were doing, and I was intrigued. I was youthfully content to walk my dogs out to the crash site if necessary to help them find the long-sailing wounded bird. Bena, by the nature of her long running and quartering, came to take hand signals more by accident than design. I could see my age coming, and that long run skill could be useful in the future.

I worked in the outdoor industry at retail and then at the wholesale and manufacturing level for more than thirty-five years. Writers' camps in the industry were one way to help outdoor writers with content for their media outlets, and it gave the manufacturers credible exposure. On one of these efforts in northeast Colorado, on a spring snow goose hunt, I was introduced to Quiny. She was the forty-five-pound black Lab that partnered with Mike Adams, owner of Web Feet Down Outfitters.

We had a crazy good shoot that first morning. If it had not been the justification of a conservation population control effort, I would have had a twinge of guilt for the number of birds we shot. If you are a nonhunter exploring these words, you may be asking yourself, "How is killing a large number of snow geese a conservation effort?" The snow geese are literally eating themselves out of house and home in their nesting areas in Canada. They are truly their own worst enemies, and they run the risk of crashing their species if a population control isn't installed. For the most part, they have no natural predators in number that could help "balance" their populations. So, there are liberal bag limits for hunters on these geese as they migrate south to winter and move back north in the spring. Possibly it will not be enough in the end. All we can do is our part. With that said, it is a specialized effort that requires specialized efforts and equipment.

I was most impressed with Web Foot Down's specialization when I saw Mike ask Quin to run from Colorado to Nebraska to pick up a wounded goose! OK, maybe it was not quite into Nebraska. The fields were really flat, and there was very little corn stubble to block the line of sight. The dog is closer to the ground than you are, so there was no way she knew where she was headed. She just ran the line when she was sent. At three hundred yards, she pulled up and looked back to Mike for more help.

Mike was in a white smock, which helped her see the signal as he shot his arm high into the air, and off she went again. I know what 235 yards looks like off my property's back fence line. Quiny finished up just shy of twice that! *Yeah, I'm going to teach Hope to do that.* I tucked what I learned into the mind drawer. Kevin's dog had run hundred-yarders, but this was close to four times that! As an outfitter's dog, Quiny gets lots of practice.

There was one other thing I noticed about Quin, and I asked Mike about it. Quiny picked up the wounded geese first. She'd be working a spread of more than three hundred decoys and somehow would pick out the wounded geese from the dozen or so that would hit the ground during a barrage of fire. They were not all up and walking around either. Some were, but she'd grab the hiders that would still have enough gas to try to walk off and had hunkered down to hide.

"You just can't teach that," Mike replied.

Awe, the mystery of wonder; should it last long.

Josh Noble is a territorial rep for a major waterfowling goods company. When I met Josh, he was a partner with a little black Lab that was fifty-two pounds wringing wet. Her name was Teal. I got to know Josh through bowfishing. Later, our company would help him with design and production of products for a bowfishing company he started. On a snow goose hunt, our marketing guy hatched the idea that our brand, Josh and I could hold our own writers' camps. The three of us went to work on that effort. It would help the company Josh worked for and our company too. Josh had a good link to some of the equipment we would need, and I had a link to the ranch. It could help the ranch operation as well. Our marketing guy would gather up the industry invites.

Josh owned an airboat and had built a set of custom pink earmuffs out of shooting muffs to help protect Teal's hearing from the engine noise. It was a natural fit to have Josh and his waterfowling brand help us and our brand on writers' camps. We had some of the best "desert" waterfowling right out our back door. The first time I saw Teal go to work was on the Great Salt Lake. The shooters were laid out in plastic coffins/sleds. They wore dark clothes and hid among five hundred black silhouettes of ducks. In the center, you laid a line of full-bodied decoys that the ducks would see and key on as they got closer to the raft of black. The object was to finish the ducks on the blocks. Teal laid in the middle of all this, behind the shooters, on an elevated stand just at the water level. It was important that she lay down—and stay that way—until the shooting was over. Then she would be called on to work the longer falling or sailing birds. Usually, a couple hunters popped up and out with Teal to fetch the closer ones.

It was a crazy hunt. Flat, flat, flat—and miles of it. The airboats were parked off maybe four or five hundred yards, and we would stage a lunch off of them. I was the chef and product demonstrator. When you shot your limit, or just got hungry, you could get out of the water and eat on the airboat. I got to do a lot of watching with the "binos." It was really fun to watch and beat the feathers out of being in the office on a desk! But, most importantly, it got us ink for our products—a bunch of it. It was a ton of work. They were usually three-day events, and you were a zombie when it was over. It was long days and short nights.

I'd usually get in the coffins on the last run before pickup or when a boat ran a group back into the dock. Being in the middle of the Great Salt Lake with no boats around is a feeling every waterfowler deserves to feel once. And with no commotion but you and a camera guy, the duck shooting was unreal. My best with a pump gun was a limit of seven in eight shots in just under twelve minutes! When I could triple with the pump on springing teal, I promised myself an autoloader.

Teal was a showstopper. She would deliver the duck to Josh and then go again. On the last duck, she'd get on the platform—sometimes without being told. Again, I thought, *How did she know it was the last duck?* It was fun to watch through the binos. I once watched her lope out on a 250-yard retrieve. The spoonie gave her trouble; it dove and dove and dove and dove. The water was only a foot deep at the most, and there was six to ten inches of mud in some places. This went on for six timed minutes.

Toward the end of the shoot, she had to lope a couple hundred yards to get to the duck. She most likely had already picked up forty ducks, give or take. There was no quit in her, and she kept after it until it was done. Everyone on the boat was watching and giving play-by-play, and there was a cheer when she finally caught the duck. Teal hatched stories of other great dogs the group members had been around. It sucked when it came to an end.

One day, I was talking with Josh via phone. He was hunting pheasants in Nebraska. He said, "Teal is here just to pick 'em up. She doesn't really know what finding and flushing them is about."

"And why would she?"

"She is geared to watch it fall and get it back. She is letting the other dogs do the hard stuff."

Teal is a constant companion of Josh. She goes everywhere with him, and he is always taking time to stop and work her in someplace conducive. Sporting dogs just love to work. A reward for them is more work! You have some responsibility to monitor that for them. I believe there is such thing as burnout. Everyone and all living creatures get tired—with maybe the exception of bugs. Sporting dogs just want to please.

Josh and I exchanged photos of our dogs and their doings. He once sent me a photo of a limit of doves laid out on the hood of his duck-scouting car. Teal sat with them on the hood. Not to be outdone, I sent him a photo of Hope on the top of the cab of an old Chevy pickup truck. I had to get her to climb clear to the top to at least tie because I had no bird in the photo. Sporting dog owners can be a little like soccer moms.

I was headed out on the lake with Josh on a hunt, and we bumped into someone he knew. He shut the boat down to discuss some conservation effort they were both involved in. A photographer from back East was out photographing the lake with the other guy, and Teal had her pink muffs on.

"Is this the dog Teal?" the camera guy asked.

It was shutter time. Josh isn't much for brimmed hunting caps with Velcro adjustments, but I noticed the skullcap he wore sat a bit taller on his head for the rest of the day. In terms that the curious nonhunter can understand, it would be like someone asking you about your child and a last-second goal in sports or some academic achievement.

Josh has a circle of friends that all run small black Labs. I got in the club more by accident of association than design. The replacement for Hope was to be another small black Lab. They don't take up much room in the boat, on the bed, or on the couch—yeah, I've softened. They can fit in the cab of the truck with three humans. They can get up on plane when they swim, which is fun to observe. They are always athletic. They don't eat much. There's not much to hide if the blind is skimpy. I'm not sure waterfowl spooks off of black movement coming late out of the decoys on a retrieve.

Best-laid plans. I ended up with a yellow "straw dog" that we will consider later in this writing. I've applied for a waiver on my membership in the club—based on the fact that the mother of the yellow is black—and a portion of the pup, some of the tail, is black. Her mentor, Hope, is also a member in good standing.

Teal has a pup to mentor now. Ravin is the newest member of the group. There is another hard day or two on the horizon.

Chapter 18

ONE IS ENOUGH?

After Coke's passing, there was a noticeable difference in Hope. She got clingy. She went everywhere with me and us. She spent time with my mother—even on her furniture. She rode in the car, and she was only crated if she was muddy. If the boat went, she went. If I had a newbie project to take bowfishing, I might leave her home for the sake of safety. Other than that reason, she usually laid under the shooting deck on the bow of the boat. She leaned out sometimes when we got shooting—she didn't need to take an arrow in the back of the head. She would whine when we went over fish. The finder showed that to be true. These fish were on the bottom in twelve feet of water. Go figure! She hated when I catfished in the fall. She'd get all wound up, and when I'd put the fishing poles in the boat, she immediately put on the grump slump. There is always a lull between the opener and migration on the pond I hunt. You can stay home, look at birdless skies, or fish. Hope hated to fish in the fall.

If Hope had a downfall, it was her coat on late-season waterfowl. She just didn't have the thick coat that my other Labs have had. I'd take steps to keep her as dry and as warm as possible for long days on the river. That usually meant a vest, a chamois for wiping off her legs, and an old duck coat to drape over her. If it was below forty degrees, I took a closed foam shop pad for her to sit on. At thirty-two degrees and below, the heater went with us. I used the same keep-her-warm methods on bank or boat. Hunting from shore did allow her to move around some.

I know some folks don't recommend feeding a dog right before a hunt. I usually feed heavier going into the season, during, and the night before a day hunt. I bring a can of tuna and some dog food and feed small portions throughout the day. Hey, I snack, and then I eat at noon—and I don't jump in the water at thirty degrees. I just don't feed it heavy all at once. It seems to make a difference in her performance and comfort. As she and I both have gotten older, the twenty-two-degree full days on the river are fewer and shorter.

Being able to get all the work in has certainly paid off for Hope becoming the best she can be—despite her trainer. There are just too many experiences to write. Since I don't want to bore you, I'll pick a few highlights. As you most likely have figured out by now, I'm not the most tech-savvy person. I have photos, but they are scattered hither and yon on zip drives and slides. Some are prints from slides, so if you have seen photos in the book, we figured it out—or someone did.

I've always had specific recall about things I witness. I think maybe bowhunting helped me with that as well; there are so many critical details one needs to pay attention to, to get the venison to the freezer once you place an arrow in the animal. I have forgotten so many of the instances of birds to the hand because they became so commonplace, but a few will always stand out. I'll relate these short stories in this chapter.

A VERSATILE DOG

Don't miss! Don't think about it! This went through my head about ten times before I let Hope out of the crate. She was five months old, and this was her maiden field voyage on live birds. OK, so they were set live birds, but they were live and would fly. I'd had them plant four chukar partridges eighty yards apart along the creek and field edge. They marked them with orange flagging tape. I just had to wait for the wind to shift before I could work crosswind, and that would push them toward the field when Hope got them up. I'd brought the Savage Fox .20-gauge with an ounce of number sixes loaded in each barrel. It was my upland go-to gun. I pointed it, and things died. It was as comfortable as good socks. The set looked good for Hope's learning—except for the head game I was playing with myself.

I had let Hope play in front of me and encouraged her out when we went for walks. I'd hide the small, scented dummy, go get her, and play "hunt 'em up." I'd stay close and get to it before she could pick it up, and then I'd praise her. I'd toss it and tell her to fetch. We had introduced the gun on walks—but not with this scenario. There is always a lot riding on the intro to live birds. No matter what method you use to introduce them, you want the dog to have a happy motivational experience.

We started toward the first marker. I lined out so we would come in about twenty yards off and into the crosswind. Hope was tight to me, maybe ten feet, when we hit the scent path. She took it, carefully tested the wind, and worked into the bird. I was a bundle of nerves. I was contemplating letting the first one fly off because I was afraid of the reaction the explosion of wings might bring and then the gun blast right behind that. I decided to see what she did when the bird broke. If she reacted with fear, I'd hold the shot. Her head had to have been right over it when it got up. She stood and watched it go. The sight picture came together, and the bird bounced a couple times in the cut hay and came to a stop.

Hope was looking at it with her ears up. She looked back at me as if to say, "Well?"

"Fetch up!"

That got me another look, and time stood still. Then she trotted off to the bird. I had yet to breathe. She messed with it, finally got it into her mouth, and trotted back to me with it.

My mind said, "One!"

Another voice said, "Three to go—don't miss. You're going to miss!" In the training and development world of human resources, they call that little voice "Self One." There are only horns on this little personage's head. It's the same little creep that causes athletes to drop a pop fly in baseball, miss both free throws off the front of the rim, and drop the last arrow in an NFAA perfect indoor round. You see, Self Two knows how to do these things. After years of experience and practice, it's just a small matter of "letting it happen."

Bird one was now in the bag, and we were approaching bird two. It went pretty much like bird one, but it took the long barrel to knock it in place with the earth. The bird came up off the ground in better form this time, and the gait out and back had another few RPMS to them.

Bird three did a bit of a "tip twist and fade right." I pushed hard to catch it, taking the motion from its wings. Hope loped to gather it up and return it. By now, she was into the game. She was panting and excited, looking out, moving off a few feet and then coming back. Money!

On bird four, I got this idea to come in upwind and then let Hope monkey around until she got downwind and the scent on it. By then, Self One was a thing of the past. We got upwind of the marker, and I stood ready, off about ten yards.

Hope messed around and got downwind. Nothing! What?

Pretty soon, she lined out nose to the ground and sucked up dander. The bird was walking and figuring it out. When the bird got up, it flew straightaway. The issue was the creek. It was about sixty feet wide, and I rushed the shot to kill the bird on this side of it. Instead, I crippled it, and it went down in the creek. *%$@$! Perfect run, and I choked it. ^&%#, Self One!* The grass was high, and I was sure it had made the creek and was floating away. About then, I heard the splash! I got to the edge in time to see Hope climbing out downstream with the bird in her mouth.

She was on her way. If it had feathers, Firestorm's Hoping for Feathers wanted it!

INTRODUCTION DUCK

We had a big snowfall in October. We had not been working on waterfowl yet in Hope's first year other than pitching winged dummies with scent. The ranch had been open to shooting for a month and a half, and we'd had a couple good days on pheasant working there. The ranch wasn't usually open to shoot on Sunday, but I could hunt any leftovers then from the weekly hunts. This particular day, I thought I'd just take Hope solo after a foot of new snow and see if we could mop up some lost birds. I was carrying my Stoeger Uplander .12-gauge side-by-side. We were hunting along some cottonwood trees and brush by the creek. Since the ranch had been quiet that day, I decided to hunt with steel shot in the event that we jumped some mallards along the creek.

We'd not hunted too long when a dozen mallards broke from the river. They came across in front of us, left to right. I picked out the last drake and slapped the modified trigger, and out of the air he came. He hit in an open field but went out of sight in the snow. Hope came up out of the willows at about the same time. She had cleared them in time and had seen the duck fall. She bounced out to the divot made in the snow where the duck had fallen.

Awesome, first duck retrieve—an easy one too!

She dug around in the snow, and the drake popped to the surface—and then it took off across the top of the snow. It was running and flapping in circles, but Hope was hot on it.

This is great practice—in pursuit!

Hope was gaining, even with the challenge of deep snow, and then the duck just flew off! Up and away off the ranch! It flew east, never really gaining good altitude and then finally out of sight. We stood and watched it go. I don't know. I have no clue—didn't then and don't now! I can't recall the first duck she brought to hand, but I remember the first one she didn't. I worried what that might do to her confidence. I worried too much, but it didn't matter. The failure may have instilled more drive. There have been hundreds of ducks delivered since then. Maybe that experience helped seal the deal because she wants feathers bad!

THE LITTLE THINGS THAT TELL YOU

Hope was a year and a half and into her first full waterfowl season. Riley and I were invited to go on a hunt with a couple guys from work. A friend of theirs was putting it together. I had introduced both of my coworkers to waterfowling, and one to hunting in general. I didn't know much about the guy who had invited us to come along. I did know *of* him. He would have his boat, and I would have mine. From the looks of his equipment, he was a seasoned waterfowler.

Toward the end of the Coke era, I had introduced a duck boat into our waterfowling efforts. I had always wanted a duck boat of my own. While Spud's partner, Dale, was one of the finest captains I may ever motor with, I just wanted my own boat. Then, I could decide when I wanted to scare the stuffing out of myself! Riding up on plane with Dale into the pitch-black, back and forth and through the maze of vegetation with only a flashlight to lead the way in his one hand and the steering wheel in his other, was always an on-edge experience! I had done it so many times that it should have felt commonplace, but some obstacle always popped up to keep your stomach near your throat! I found that lying in the bottom of the boat with the decoys and a prayer always distorted my fears.

My drive to be a captain was furthered by a borrowed boat from work that we had used as part of an R&D project. It was a V hull with a motor that didn't quite fit, but motoring across water continued to drive my appetite. I finally got enough saved up to get a true duck boat. Boats add a whole different angle to the outdoor life. They say that the best days of boat ownership are the day you purchase it and the day you sell it. I will admit they can be a challenge to deal with. Fuel, electronics, and water are not necessarily compatible. I justified the purchase with my home boss (the wife) from a "multiple-use" angle of fishing, hunting, and eventually grandkid relationship building. I'm now on my third boat. (Yeah, you outgrow them, honey?) I run Mud Buddy motors and have been told by the dealer where I purchased it that they know of no other customers with the amount of hours I have on the motor in the period of time I've had them. If dogs love trucks, they *really* dig boats!

We were going to hunt a place where the water was crotch-deep on an average person. That put water to my belly button. The dogs would work out of the boats. This would be Hope's maiden voyage in this situation. She was familiar on dry land and a couple late-summer practices in water, getting into the boat by using the portable dog dock. You attached it to the boat for the purpose of assisting the dog into and out of the boat in deep water. There were going to be a lot of new things. I just planned that something may go haywire and worked to get my head right to deal with it.

We had positioned the boats per direction of our host. He had all the decoys, and they put those out while we piddled around and organized our boat for the anticipated shooting to come. The other boat was positioned twenty yards to our left, facing west. We were facing slightly south, positioned on the northern end of the spread. Just at legal time, while the other boat was finalizing the organization and person positioning, a group of gadwalls came in and flared from their movements up and over us.

I was the only one ready, and I dumped a big drake just behind the boat. Hope was not positioned out on the dog deck. She was down inside the boat, but from the plop, she knew where the duck was. She promptly made an exit hole out the back of the boat by the motor. I wasn't exactly happy that she broke before I sent her, but she accomplished the goal: bird to the hand. I had to coax her around to find the dog dock. She returned to where she had left from and couldn't climb in because she couldn't get her hind legs on anything to push her up and out of the deep water. Grabbing her by the vest and lifting her in would have taught her nothing.

Within a few minutes, another group of ducks worked directly into the other boat's end of the spread. They shot a couple that fell out in front of them and beyond the decoys. The next thing I knew, our host was walking out to the ducks with his dog swimming beside him. *I guess that is how you do it out here.* It made a bit of sense since hard land was a ways away, and I could see how a dog could get confused in the maze of small tulles islands and possibly get lost. I was the newbie to this situation and was on the watch-and-learn curve. I always error on the side of caution in case of risk, and I could see how losing a dog out there would be problematic.

A big group of mallards finally bought the setup and worked to set down in the hole. We tore into them. Three fell off our boat just north of us in an open area. I made sure Hope had a mark on one and then sent her. I repeated it on the second bird. The third bird had drifted a bit long. I took the second bird from her as she hit the dog deck. She didn't wait for the mark; she just bailed off like a sprint swimmer making a turn, and back she went. She got to the edge but had lost the mark. She started to swim back, and I threw her a hand signal. She hung a left and swam twenty yards to pick up the duck. How she remembered there was a third duck back there is still a mystery to me.

We shot a few more ducks, and the retrieving was not so challenging. The shooting slowed. Lunch was happening when the seasoned waterfowler ask me how old Hope was.

"Really?" he said. "Who trained her?"

"Well, Ri and I are working on it," I replied.

"Really? Maybe you should train mine."

I was wearing a stocking cap that day and didn't need to expand the Velcro. Hope made up for what little my kid and I knew about boat-hunting waterfowl. It was a small comment on a big deal for us just getting into the methodology of hunting out of a boat.

The day drew long after lunch. Naps were happening in the warming November sun. At about three o'clock, our host left my workmates with us and sped to the dock. He returned with two youths and their father. We were a few minutes off that last hour that usually has a few birds in the air prior to closing time. Several more boats began to show up in the area around us. We were about to witness a remarkable event.

Utah is one of the few places you can hunt tundra swans. You must draw a permit to do so. We had seen one swan shot earlier in the day by a group hunting four hundred yards from us. It was high—or what I call "tall." I maybe thought it was too tall, but with one shot, the swan fell stone-dead. At that distance, I could see the water column reaching ten feet into the air on splashdown. I knew that adventure would have to be on our agenda in the future. Forty-five minutes before closing time, the sky lit up with swans. Their calls were noisy, which added to the commotion. The birds were quite gregarious and responded well to the four or five swan decoys we had around the spread of ducks. The youths each shot one. Both fell close to the boat, one within reach, and the human retriever fetched up the other. I witnessed ten shot that day by those lucky few who had drawn the tag. The commotion was crazy for about forty-five minutes.

Our host ran the youths and one of our guys back to the dock, and the rest of us gathered up the decoys. There was an amazing sunset that night. It was early November, and the temps dropped quickly. Our host returned to ferry decoys. Hope had done the lion's share of the duck retrieving and was "give out." I took her out of her damp vest and put her inside a gear bag. I zipped her in, and she stayed there until we reached the dock. No muss, no fuss—just glad to be there.

In the back of my head, I thought, *Can a forty-five-pound pup retrieve a swan?*

On the Mark, Get Set, Hope!

I've had a couple of "what the hell was that?" moments with Hope. She isn't perfect, but I am pretty sure they were brought on by my flawed training. Oddly enough, something good seems to come from those initial moments of pause. If not right then, then later.

I was guiding an outdoor writer at the ranch, and he clean missed a bird. He will go nameless because it too was a mystery. He is the finest shotgun swinger I'd ever witnessed. The bird sailed to the top of the ridge, barely clearing it and out of sight. We all watched it go. To Hope, I'm pretty sure it looked like it fell into the hill at the top from her view, just over the tops of the weeds. I said, "No bird!"

For some reason, she stood, watched, and then broke! There was no turning or stopping her. Over the ridge she went. I could see for a long ways south after I topped the ridge, but I was out of gas from long days and just let her go. Ten long minutes later, she came trotting back up the road from the direction we had hunted with her tongue dragging to the ground. I wasn't happy, and she knew it. After a drink, we picked up where we had left off and moved on. The guys had missed very few birds that day, and maybe she just thought it was down or thought "no" was "go." Whatever, it happens.

She made up for it the day of the inaugural shoot of the new driven hunt simulator. It was designed as best it could be, all things considered, to mimic an English-driven pheasant shoot. On an English shoot, the shooter stands in an open field position with other shooters. There are maybe thirty to forty yards between each shooter. The shooter has a dog and possibly a dog handler at hand. Beaters or drivers come walking through the woods toward the shooters. The birds hopefully flush in the direction of the shooters, up and over the treetops, and into the range of the guns. The birds usually have a good head of steam as they break into the clear, and the shooting isn't as easy as it might sound.

The ranch-modified version gave the shooter a shooting frame or window to shoot from to form safe shooting zones. The birds were released above and in front of the shooters off the top of a ridge that basically was like the birds clearing the treetops. At this outdoor writers' camp, everyone insisted that the ranch owner be the first person to shoot a bird off the new setup. The pressure to perform well in those types of events never seems to allow it to go well. It's like christening a ship with a bottle that refuses to break! There was a lot of positive heat put on him to be the first. After all, it was his gig, on his property, and he had just purchased a brand-new CZ over-and-under .28-gauge. That was enough to "brave him up." Yes, even retired colonels can get nerves. I don't recall that missing was something he ever did. The odds were now stacked to where it could go either way. I stood by with Hope and held my breath for what was about to take place.

Out came the bird. Bang! Clean miss. Bang! The bird didn't fold, but it faltered enough that I knew it had taken lead. It sailed two hundred yards across a hayfield and into the outside corner of some bent but standing corn where the two fields met.

There was a lot of supportive bantering of the "it happens" type. I heard a "that bird is lost" comment from the group. I looked down at Hope, and I knew she had the mark!

"Nope that bird is hit—a glider," I said. To add pressure to the cause, but wanting to save some face for the colonel, I said, "Back." *What the hell was I thinking? Eight writers from all the major outdoor media magazines, and I may have confirmed the miss if she doesn't find it. I may have just added injury to insult!*

The black rocket almost cleared the thirty-foot-wide creek and was up and out in a bounce! Still on a line, hard charging away and gaining speed, she raced. My stomach climbed into my throat and was cutting off my air. She disappeared into the corner's edge. *Find it please.*

I saw the bird jump above the corn and meet up with a black shadow that shot up from under it. *Man, that was awesome!*

She loped back to us. Bailing into, then out of, the creek, she didn't stop to shake and deliver the still-live bird to my hand. It was only then that I became conscious of the camera shutter sounds and others moving around us.

I don't know exactly how many birds she picked up that day off the driven event or in the field, but it was a bunch. She wasn't getting any retrieval help from the shorthair pointer that had showed up on the driven hunt to help in the field hunt. His handler said that he didn't retrieve. Uh, yeah? Well, OK then! She got a hand from the writers waiting to shoot if the birds fell close. Lots of feathers help build good dogs, and I have been lucky to be involved with some. For Hope, well, it's in her DNA—and she loves it!

THE REFUSAL

I'd done it. Finally! I had gotten lucky and drawn one of the few cache crane tags! When my brother started hunting sandhill cranes in northeastern Idaho, I quietly responded, "Must we shoot everything?" Really? And I'm a hunter? What was up with that thinking?

My father hated the great blue heron/blue crane, as he called the fish-gobbling menace. He'd seen one too many of them toss down his favorite fishing target: the cutthroat trout. He wasn't a fan of pelicans either. Those bucket mouths most likely did more damage to local trout populations than the blue cranes did. And we now know, based on studies the Idaho Fish and Game have conducted, that places like the Blackfoot Reservoir in eastern Idaho truly have a problem between the native cutthroat trout and the pelicans. I remember him scolding me one day when a BC flew off as we arrived at a favorite fishing hole. He told me that if I was ever arrested for shooting a blue crane that he would bail me out and buy me another box of ammo. I had to chew on that comment a lot over the years. So, maybe that built into me that cranes—regardless of feather colors—were problematic and should be avoided. And while I understood his dislike and heard it a bunch, I was in a jail cell once. I had them lock me in while I worked on a scout project of painting the jail. Didn't like it—not one bit! So, from me, cranes had always gotten a pass.

I had started to research the sandhill crane once my brother started to rave about the taste. He proved it by saying, "Here, try this." The jerky was incredible!

I also looked into the damage that a flock of twenty could do to a standing grainfield. With five-inch-wide feet and a wingspan of five feet, they destroyed more grain than they ate getting in, out, and around in the field. Land a hundred cranes in that same field, and it would look like the cattle got in there.

The tags were being offered on a limited basis as a depredation issue solution, and I was able to justify hunting one season with my brother and his family. They had the hunt methodology down to a small science, but I still found it to be no walk in the park. You just gain a whole new outlook for the things you pursue to become your diner. Things had to line up just right to take down the "ribeye of the sky." You would be hard-pressed to tell the difference between grilled sandhill crane breast and a cut of tender beef sirloin! They are delicious. They are amazingly smart and annoying at the same time. During your pursuit to plate them, your respect level goes up in a hurry. You want the landowner to be happy, but you don't want them all to go away at the same time. I guess helping with balance is the best you can do as a hunter.

There are very few crane tags available in the Cache Valley of Northern Utah, which is where I live. East and west of us, in Rich and Box Elder Counties, the Utah Division of Wildlife offers more tags based on Crane populations and crop damage. Most of the hunting is done on private land, and getting permission isn't difficult. In the first weeks of October, the cranes stage behind my house. One day, they just start to lift off, circling up to a distance where they resemble sand particles, and then they are gone— headed south. Their call in the spring is listened for starting on March 1. That is a sign that winter will soon lose its grip. They wave goodbye to summer and say hello to spring. Sorry you can't all witness it. As a matter of fact, it is October 10 today, and they are staging out back.

If you are reading this and don't hunt, what I'm about to say may sound odd. If I had never hunted them, I would have never fully understood or respected them. Sorry, you just can't get the full picture unless you are all in. "I do not hunt just to kill. I kill to say I have hunted." Jose Ortega Gasset, a Spanish philosopher, made this statement in the 1500s, and it is still a sound comment today.

I had drawn the tag. That was the first step, and I had a plan. Boy, did I have a plan! You see, one of my justifications for owning a duck boat was to get better access for shooting the evasive species of common carp on our Cutler Reservoir using bowfishing tackle. I shoot a bunch of them. Cut 'em, sink 'em, and feed 'em to the catfish. Carp are not part of the native water systems in the US. They are an invasive species brought here with possibly a good intent that went south in a hurry! Carp constantly feed by rooting the bottom of waterways, lakes, and ponds. The water in lakes and ponds can remain muddy, and no photosynthesis can take place for structuring of vegetation. Shorebirds and waterfowl suffer because of it—and so do many species of fish. During my hours of being out there on "the pond," bowfishing or angling with rod and reel, I get to observe lots of things.

This year, I paid particular attention to where the cranes transitioned from roost to the feed store. I was pretty sure I was going to be the only person to drop a crane in the pond. It was a fairly new hunt to the valley, and I didn't know of anyone who had shot one over water. The hunting was usually done in and around fields. While cranes will decoy, most of them in our region get shot as they fly by, heading in or out of the fields to eat.

The night before the hunt opened, you'd have thought it was going to be my first deer hunt. I didn't sleep well. I had the boat geared up and attached to the truck the night before. I just had to jump Hope into the cab, and we were headed to the launch. Fifteen minutes before shooting time, I edged the boat along the cattails' west-facing edge. The cranes would be coming from the east. The cattails were eight feet tall. The cranes would never see me until it was too late!

There is no doubt when they wake up in the morning. They are noisy. Their call urgency changes just before they get into the air. The first crane went by south of me, out of range, and then four more came. I immediately went into the "wrong guess mentality," but I fought to stay put. They had used this point every day for the past two weeks. Then I heard what sounded like some coming in line. I wouldn't see them until they were on me because I couldn't see above the wall of vegetation I was hiding against. It got louder and louder. Then they were there, passing north of me, thirty yards out. There were five in a line.

One thing I'd learned about cranes was how fast they move. They look like they are not because they are so gangly and strung out, but they cruise. I swung up for the last bird, pushed the bead up on the second bird's tail feathers, and pulled the trigger. The last bird came apart. Nothing falls as awkwardly from the sky as a crane. Splashdown! I'd done it, but it wasn't as clean as I'd have liked. Its head was still up. So, I got the boat together to motor out and finish up my sloppiness. I wasn't sending Hope on a wounded crane. That beak could take out an eye. I'd seen their attitude when wounded on field hunts. I eased the boat toward it, killed the motor, floated to a stop—as required by law when shooting from a boat—and finished off the crane.

Hope was pretty close to exploding. I picked up the camera, made sure it was on video, pointed, and said, "Hope."

She launched from the boat and came up on plane—and I had it all on camera! *This is great! Proof that I am truly out on the pond plus a retrieve on camera to boot!* She got to the crane, swam around it, looked left and right, and then started back to the boat. *What?* "Hope, no, fetch it up!"

Nope, not going to happen! She got to the boat and climbed up on the pod.

I lined her out again and said, "Hope."

She just sat there.

Then I thought if I got her to swim by it another time, maybe it would kick in. I said, "Back!"

She climbed down into the boat, and it remains a mystery to me to this day. She has dug numerous pheasants out of the water. My panic of a good video going bad was all caught on my camera as she swam back to the boat. Funny! Maybe she knew what would happen, and since I was finally videoing one, she wanted to see me come unglued on tape. I was concerned that I had an answer to my swan question. Maybe she wouldn't bring one. Maybe they were just too big. But the crane didn't weigh any more than a goose, and while challenged by a goose's size on land, she ferries them fine in the water.

Well, I think I'm maybe the only person to drop a crane in the pond anyway. I can be unique in my own mind.

BUILDING A RIVER DOG

I told my son that, most likely, we were not giving some of the local rivers the respect they deserved for waterfowling, and we started down a path to expand our horizons. Much of the migration feed lines had changed migration patterns in northern Utah, western Wyoming, and eastern and southern Idaho, but there was still some migration that followed the remaining feed line. The water systems remained relatively the same for the migration.

Growing up and prior to my teen years, I never hunted waterfowl over water other than to jump small creeks and ponds where we could retrieve the bird by wading or waiting till the wind helped the dead birds float to shore. Most of our waterfowl hunting was in the harvested barley fields, and we used a minimal spread of decoys.

My father was a railroader, and since the tracks followed farmlands and rivers, he could observe waterfowl feeding in certain fields. Permission to hunt was easy to get in the community we grew up in and around. To coin a modern hunting phrase, we were on the X—most all the time. Six decoys were just enough to take the fowls' attention to a focus and allow my father to get his gun up—and later an awkward twelve-year-old and his gun—without them flaring adversely out of range. Our hides were mostly standing by a big fence post. Sometimes we built a bale blind of straw or used tumbleweeds. Gear was minimal, but the farm roads usually allowed us to drop off our gear by the setup. Those days of ease and consistency, for the most part, are gone. More and more private land hunting opportunity is being gobbled up by the almighty dollar. We had intentions to carry our gear beyond a fence line and pick up and drop off in order to find better shooting opportunities on public lands.

I had found some decoys by a company called FUD at the SHOT show. Everything about them made sense to me for applications of mobility. After some use, I found the metal arm that was used to hold them together when folded out to maybe be overkill. I also understood production and the quantity of scale to help keep costs in price points of consumer acceptability. The cost of producing a nylon arm may have pushed the product out of its acceptable consumer price parameters. Being metal, it could be used as a field or as a bank spike more readily. And the anchor could be built of the same materials. It did have more weight, which kind of flew in the face of their intentions of light weight. As compared to full-body decoys, they did reduce space consumed and weight. We could carry two dozen as easily as a half a dozen full bodies hiking into the river system we planned to hunt. I really wanted to find an X, and that alone would reduce our gear.

Simplifying the effort to hike in hunting anywhere for anything is always a key consideration. You need room to carry the birds back out. Some of the areas required us to hike in to observe what was actually taking place as it pertained to waterfowl usage, and if we were going to be there, we might as well sit it. The next issue that loomed heavy for me was putting Hope in current. It would, and it did cause me stress. We gave up shooting opportunities in order to keep the birds falling where pickup was safe. However, flowing water and a downed duck in sight oftentimes overruns a dog's ability to hear a command. So, scouting out possible hazards for the dog was of the utmost importance.

On our first hunt, in October, I learned that my FUD solutions just didn't take much current well. So, imitating a couple ducks that had just set and were working their way into the rest of the spread was off the list. They also were a challenge to recover to their floating position even in quiet pools when the dog ran through them and hit the anchor lines. All the above management considerations relate to how the dog becomes. Hope was taught to float on her second season.

I was pretty sure she wasn't going to run off. She was chipped if she were to get lost as a backup, but I wanted her collar with her ID off of her to minimize the chances of her hanging up on brush in the river. I'd played that hung-up game with Dolly once, besides the ice hole adventure, and I really didn't want to travel those experiences again. I knew I'd eventually have to figure out how to include and/or get over her using a vest on the river in later-season hunts. The vests often have built-in conveniences to help handle the dog, but they could be a deadly disadvantage in some situations. The leg openings could become problematic for running a limb up in and hang them up. So, we will cross those bridges as we approach them.

We had a good experience that first outing. We shot half a dozen birds with easy retrieves attached. My son shot a hermaphrodite mallard, which shows drake and hen markings. We ate it instead of preserving it on the wall. Duh! We observed a true X during that first outing, and the next week, we hiked in to see what it had to offer. There were a couple of challenges with brush in the water and a couple runs of rapids. A canoe could navigate the bounces. They would only be a challenge on wounded ducks for the dog, and we committed right then and there to hammer anything wounded into a dead float. Well, even with your best intentions, it doesn't always happen, and that adds a degree of difficulty for the dog.

When you take someone with you who might be new to the hunting situation, there is always a bit of a learning curve. You can try to shoot the duck so it will fall where it's an easy recovery. You can only do your best to explain the reasoning. The practice of it with an excited hunter makes it difficult. On this particular day, the X had changed a bit, and we had to move. This opened up more water, but there were two rapids that split an island. You had to shoot the ducks that were close so they would come down the rapid closest to you and into slower water. A long fall would mean a bigger set of rapids, taking dog and duck away and out of sight. We were still fairly new to the history of this place. The water levels had been such that I couldn't get to and scout the back of the island for floating safety. It was going pretty well. Then someone shot a goldeneye a bit long.

I love this duck. I call them mini geese because they take a bunch of killing; they are tough, fast flyers. They fly a great distance to get to us, have beautiful markings on their feathers, and seem to enjoy the roughest weather. In my teenage years, I didn't really appreciate them. They just signaled that things were freezing up—and my jump-shooting mallards was days from being over. On a scale of one to ten of my favorite ducks to eat, they score a solid four. They are very difficult to skin. They pretty much become a jerky candidate. Enough brine and smoke can solve a bunch of palate issues. As far as shooting goes, they score an eight out of nine. They fly super-fast and have feathers that are so thick and tight that pellets have a hard time penetrating the vitals. So, we try to head shoot them, which means quicker kills. You have to push yourself out on the lead way farther than you usually do for mallard ducks. That is often hard to remember to do. Even when you are a seasoned shooter, you can get lulled to sleep from shooting mallards. As a good friend of mine once said, "A seven-mile-an-hour wind and shooting decoying mallards is like shooting balloons." I'll participate every day I can! In comparison, goldeneye shooting would be like standing on third base and trying to shoot hard grounder baseballs at the short stop. I'll also purchase that participation ticket!

Dropping ducks in the right spot had been going pretty well. Then someone in our bunch wounded a golden that looked dead but a little too far out. Hope was halfway there when it righted itself and headed to the top of the larger rapid. I called Hope off, and the bird was left for the eagles. The law states that you need to make every effort to recover a wounded duck. And if you cannot recover it, you count it anyway in your limit.

When Hope got back to the bank, she and I ran downstream to the bottom of the run where the channel comes out from behind the island. The bird never showed up. Could Hope have caught up to it? I doubt it. It was a wounded diving duck, and dive they do. The sure thing was that Hope wasn't hung up in some crap and drowning out of sight of me. And she would go on to be the conservation tool she became on this river. I can count on one hand the ducks we have lost on this river in eight years of hunting it. One was the goldeneye, and one was a long flying drake mallard that flew in the direction we walked out and crumpled from a heart shot. We left it to pick up as we left, and a bald eagle beat us to it. Another drake dove and never resurfaced, and I'll add two for good measure that I cannot recall.

Once the area was completely scouted, I was comfortable letting her ride the waves, chasing the retrieve on dead and a wounded duck. I still preferred them dead—in close and dead—but once in a while, one would go long. On this particular day, I had a friend with me who was new to the drill. A pair of mallards came in front of my buddy. He shot at the hen first because she was first and missed. Then he switched to the drake and killed it clean. I was pretty sure he had hit the hen. She ran out of gas downriver, lit, and floated around the corner. The rule on wounded birds is if the head is up, spend some ammo and lay it down. The bird was much too far away to finish it off.

My friend had been all enthralled with the easy retrieve of the drake and hadn't seen the other duck glide in downriver. After Hope handed me the first bird, I sent her long downriver.

He said, "Where is she going?"

I said, "Some ducks lit around the corner. I asked her to go scare 'em back up to us."

"Ooh?" His reply dripped with confusion, wonderment, and doubt.

Hope disappeared around the corner a hundred yards downriver. She had played this game before. The water slowed there, and wounded ducks sometimes hung the edge of the river. She got to give them a "lion pounce." In about three minutes, she came trotting back up along the bank with the bird that was very much still alive in her mouth.

"I guess she couldn't turn them," I said. "Dang it, Hope. You could have at least picked out a drake!"

"I'll be dammed," my buddy said. "Whose limit does that one go on?"

I had sold it! Later, I confessed so we could stay within the law.

I'd hate to say we have gotten cocky on the river. I fight off the urge in order to ward off bad luck. However, when you hear someone who's been with you before hunting the river say to a friend they have brought along, "There she goes," as Hope blows into the water to cut off a drifter, it's tells you maybe you have arrived as a team.

Sometimes an X lights up with such commotion in this area that shooting, counting, and receiving the bird is all you're getting done. Hope is running on her own marks. There isn't even time for a quick "good girl." And if there was, she wouldn't be listening. She is at work. She owns this section of river. There are other sections I won't hunt regardless of the bird numbers. There is just too much risk involved. One of the reasons I hunt ducks is to relax. Even on this safer stretch of river, I winced a bit with uneasy wonder the first time she floated off around the corner to chase a duck.

I was hunting with a buddy on the Snake River in western Idaho one year. Our retriever beyond the pocket we were in was his twenty-four-foot Phantom jet boat. This area of the Snake doesn't necessarily have big rapids, but the water moves in places faster than it looks like it is. And it is a big, wide river. I asked him about river dogs in this area. Basically they lose a few every year to the river. He said something to the extent of, "They learn it or die."

Geez! I get it. The first time Hope floated off around a corner on our small river, I internalized it. This crew never hunts this monster Snake River without a rescue boat, and they have great dog control to help keep the dog out of harm's way. When ice floats, the dogs are relieved of duty.

I don't know much about field trials. I'm glad the exercise is there, and I'm in no way intending to disrespect the game. Hope runs very few "straight" lines on the river. She has learned to use the bank to cut distance quickly and efficiently. The dogs on the Snake River learn this as well. A work associate of mine shot his first mallard drake, and it fell in the center of the river we hunt above the split rapids. It had just a broken wing, and it headed away from us and to the opposite bank. It then started swimming upstream.

Hope was on her way but drifting slowly against the current to where she would come out some distance below the duck that continued to move upstream. When Hope got out, she was sixty yards below the bird. She didn't stop to shake; she just hit the afterburners and railed upriver using the bank to gain position.

The bird put on the best speed it could.

I didn't see Hope even slow to launch. She left the three-foot bank and lit squarely on the drake with an eruption of water (her lion pounce). She popped to the surface, started back across the river at a slow drift, and exited on our side about twenty yards upstream. Over time, I saw her do some amazing things on the river that the nature of the beast had taught her. You just can't teach some of the things they do. And one of those "amazing things" cost me two hundred bucks!

YOU ARE WELCOME

There had been a few pheasants around all year along the river. One rooster had an extremely long tail. One evening, he showed up behind us as we were waiting on the ducks. I tried to slowly maneuver from our hide to get open enough for a shot when it flushed. I showed Hope the hand to stay put. I thought I'd have a better chance just rushing it, and I didn't want to risk tangling Hope in my feet. That went south in a hurry. It was almost duck thirty, and I didn't want to complicate it with a pheasant chase. (Excuse me for my lack of execution. I think Hope bought it.)

A couple weeks later, a coworker and I were on the river with a couple youths. There was no X that day. The migration had slowed. The kids were out of school on break, so we took them for that reason. School sure seems to get in the way of life schooling nowadays. Anyway, Hope and I were downriver on the end of the set. I always run Hope of the end of the drift to give her more time to get to multiple retrieves before the last rapid. It was maybe ten o'clock, and the sun had been warming us for a bit. That place will sometimes light up at about eleven, so we had decided to hang till noon. Upriver, we had dropped a sleigh with a portable stove and oven on it. After we discussed the plan for the remainder of the time, my coworker bushwhacked it behind me upriver to cook some orange rolls for river brunch.

I had taken the round from my barrel and laid my gun aside. Hope was sitting there with that bored look she gets from time to time. I had just removed my coat when I heard the cackle and wingbeat of a rooster pheasant working up through the cottonwoods and coming my way. It cleared the treetops, heading across river, and I got a shell racked in and the gun mounted. The 1¼ oz. of #3 Black Cloud meant for ducks, released the birds' spirit and left the dinner portion of it. It hit the opposite bank about sixty feet up the cliff-like embankment in some brush. Hope was already on her way. When she climbed out on the opposite bank, she stood there and let the bird, which had been flapping on and off, roll the remainder of the way down the embankment to the trail she stood on between the steep bank and the river. The bird was done. I was already trying to decide if it should be fried straight up or Crockpotted. (And why hadn't Hope climbed the hill? She did it all the time on ducks.)

Hope was five years old and running most of the time on feather octane; she scooped up dead birds on the run and bailed into the ones that were alive. She didn't pounce on this bird. She just gingerly picked it up kind of by the shoulder/wing forward section of the bird. She looked back across the river at me some forty yards away and then started upriver with the bird in her mouth. For the life of me, I couldn't understand what she was doing. She had dug ducks off that trail in numbers, and then she just bailed back in and would come out a few yards below me on the drift back. She carefully waded out until she had to swim, and she drifted right to my feet. She exited the river, laid the bird down, walked off fifteen feet, and shook.

I picked up the bird. Not a feather was out of place. Its long, curly tail wasn't even wet! The bird glowed with colors I'd never observed before in the midmorning sun. Hope just stood and looked at me with a look I'd never seen before. Kind of a "well, there you go" kind of look. Two hundred dollars attached it to my wall next to a great memory photo of the team.

WE ARE DOING WHAT?

Taking a dog out of its comfort zone can be a challenge to it, your ego, and others around you. One of the reasons outfitters like Mike Adams won't let you bring a dog on a snow goose hunt is due to what I call "breaking Chi." It just upsets what he has going on: getting you the most possible shooting you can at snows. Dogs without manners in new situations have compounded issues. Dogs with dogs that don't know one another are a crapshoot; they can get along or vet bills could be waiting to happen.

So, as bad as I would have liked to run Hope on the GSL (Great Salt Lake), I was always a guest there, and those taking me had the dog power. I knew better than to ask. We had planned a teal hunt when I got the call from the airboat captain. His partner, Teal, was wounded and down. Could I bring Hope?

Well, hell yeah! Then reality began to set in. She hasn't a clue how to lay down on that dog stand. I always hunted her in a sitting position because that is just the situation we are usually in so she could see to mark fallen birds. She would be in the shadow of Teal, the queen of the GSL, and she had no experience in this situation. I wanted to vomit! The nerves came home right after I hung up. I knew how critical it was for a dog to lay quiet on that stand, having been there before a few times. Those birds can pick up a twitch and bail before they are in the death zone, and then it's watching wildlife for the day. Football that weekend would be void of Teal poppers, and that is a shame!

Hope wore Teal's airboat earmuffs. I was so on edge that I spaced that photo moment. Hope and Teal are about the same size. They both have retrieved a few ducks, but out on the lake, any commonality would cease. It was Teal's house! We found the rafts of birds we wanted to work and set up. Usually the stand is in the back of the spread, and the dog sits well away from the handler. Even for a dog that will lie down and stay put, they use larger silhouettes on longer stems to try to hide the pooch. I had them position my layout/coffin where I could hold onto Hope's collar and keep her down for as long as possible. Little did I know this day was about to cost me seven hundred dollars.

The first mob of teal came right up the death lane. I held Hope down and didn't shoot. I figured if she could get off the stand when I allowed her, bring back a bird, and then jump up on her new place, that would be some of the battle out of the way—and we'd see how it would go from there.

That worked fine. On the next group, she relaxed enough that I'd let go of her and shot. I saw her pop up as I did, but the birds were in and climbing to leave. My moving about had created a hole in the mud, and I was about to take on water down the back of my waders. It was hard to sit up to shoot with my feet above the rest of me. It required moving my coffin. Hope wouldn't lie down unless I put her there. Too much going on for her to look at, and sitting up suited her. She'd lie down, but she would pop back up as soon as the calling started. I asked the captain if it was hurting us. I was ready to kneel behind her to keep her lying and still while others shot to avoid screwing up the hunt.

He said, "Well, it isn't helping—but I don't think it's hurting."

So, I just had her sit. That seemed to work best.

I finally relaxed and was content to let her sit there as she would. Being relaxed helped my shooting. My salt gun, a Remington .887 pump, which I had put through hell, pulled a triple on teal toward the end as I caught up from my slow start. I'd promised myself that when I tripled on teal with the pump gun, I would purchase Hope an autoloader. You heard me! Enter a triple exit for seven hundred bucks. Somewhere within the thirty-five teal that rode to the dock on the airboat that day, Hope had retrieved two at the same time, a couple times, to save her efforts out and back. Ran marks to the tune of two hundred yards on wounded birds that she then had to chase down and stayed out of the way when asked as we set up and picked up. I don't think I could have asked for more.

The next day, I got out the dog stand, and in twenty minutes, I taught her to lie down away from me on the stand, fetch the bumper to me, and then get up on the stand and lie down. I sent a video to the captain. Later, he asked, "How is my other favorite little Lab doing?" I know he had other favorites, and I was happy to have Hope numbered among them.

WOW, THOSE ARE BIG!

Most of my waterfowl focus in the past several years has been on ducks. I guess it is because the action comes faster. Canada geese, in these parts, nowadays, take military-planning tactics. Timing is everything. They also put up with pressure way less than ducks do. Private land access is a key to success, and that doesn't come easy anymore. We compete here with some very large open sewage lagoons that the geese use to stay out of harm's way. The ducks share some of that location, but they seem to be more antsy and willing to move around.

While waterfowl use the river, they don't particularly feel comfortable there. It is a high-banked, deep, meandering river with few gravel and sandbars to rest on. All reaches of the impoundment of the river behind the dam are accessible, and it doesn't take geese long to learn that it isn't a place that allows resting. When the lagoons freeze over, along with all the farm ponds, the goose hunting can pick up. And at about that time, the last bump of southern headed geese will pass through.

Many geese have learned to pick out a living along the way—as long as they have open water to roost and drink. It has been interesting to watch the geese change their diet survival strategies over the years. Grains are harvested with vacuum-like precision with little waste left on the ground. Turf farms, golf courses, fall grain, and meadow grasses make up the bulk of the diet of our local geese. Depending on the type of year, as it pertains to snow and ice, we often have a few geese remain throughout the year if they are able to pick out a living. These abilities can extend as far west in our fringe of the Pacific flyway as Burley, Idaho, and as far north as Idaho Falls, Idaho, for the Canada geese. There can be some good January hunting for Canada geese in these regions, but two hard days of icing lockdown can end it. They seem to be able to work around four or so inches of snow depth, and as long as it stays warm, they stay.

All waterfowl hunting in this region, usually gets busy November 1 as a general rule. That is when you see the largest variety of ducks, a few migratory geese, and the tundra swans beginning to show up. We have to drive an hour west to get into a unit where we can swan hunt. Drawing a tag is a bit more difficult nowadays, even with the increase of the permits. You about need a bonus point at this writing. Most hunters have drawn by the third year of application. You have to take an online class before you apply. The main focus is on teaching the difference between tundra swans and trumpeter swans. Ten trumpeters checked in at the time of this writing will shut down the tundra season. That is important info, but the training doesn't do enough to educate hunters about what they are getting in to.

Some permit holders should stay home. Sorry, but they should. The swan is a big item, sixteen to twenty pounds on average, and they can take lots of killing. They are usually farther away than they look; due to size and coloration, being white, they are deceiving. Sky-busting is a huge problem during this hunt. It wounds birds, it educates them, and it affects the opportunities of hunters working to do it right.

On the Bear River Bird refuge, the Feds have limited dike-walking hunters to ten rounds of ammo. This has helped some with the sky-busting. Also, many of the local serious waterfowlers have taken it on themselves to help permit holders who have no experience. You will have way more fun if you do some homework ahead of time. Some of that homework comes with just getting out there. You do not have to pull the trigger at everything that flies by. And with that said, I will illustrate how even the best-laid plans can fall apart. I won't dis anyone who gives it their best try. But if you're slobbing it up, high on ego and the notion that drawing the permit somehow gives you the right to do it however you'd like—without regard to the ethic of it—please take up another pastime!

The first year Riley and I put in, we drew tags. We just couldn't get time and weather to line up so we could attend. I drew again the next year and almost waited too long on that permit to get there. The birds hadn't been in by number, but there was a big freeze coming that could lock up the only place I really knew to hunt at that time. I'd up graded in my fleet of boats, and the 1851 f4 Excel welded boat and Mud Buddy surface drive cut a slit through half an inch of ice to open water with way more confidence than my riveted boat.

Jason Saltern, a fairly new waterfowler, had offered to come along for the look-see as wingman. I have known Jason since he was sixteen, and I had encouraged, as of late, his participation into waterbirds. He was one of those "dusty, dry hiking bird hunters." His partner's name is Jack the Wonder Dog. Jack is also a converted water dog since Jason included him from his upland game kennel. A November wader filling while wading to retrieve a duck will motivate that. Jack swims with the best of them.

Hope, a couple dozen mixed duck decoys, Bonnie, Clyde, and Annie Oakley (the three swan decoys) rounded out the boat's load. I picked out a point with open water under one of the observed flight paths from one rest area to another, and we set up. It was the best guess of a crapshoot I could muster. It didn't take long to shoot our limits of pintail ducks. We tossed in a couple mallards and a few gadwalls because they were there for good measure. I had to keep reminding myself that we were here for a swan, and shooting ducks could mess that up. The swans usually flew the last hour of legal light. If we needed to, we would pass on ducks then.

We had finally talked ourselves out of shooting anymore ducks unless it was a canvasback! We had just knocked it off and settled in when Jason said, "I hear a swan."

We looked to the north, and a quarter mile away, we saw a lone swan. He started to drop into the flight lane. I said, "I'm going to kill that bird." There was no time to mess around being picky. Most likely, the pond would be frozen solid in two days—if not by tomorrow. The swan was on the flight path, losing elevation. At one hundred yards, the landing gear came down, and it dropped its flaps, preparing to land with the trio of fakes.

I'm not sure why I wasn't on that end of the boat, other than it was just how I stuffed it from the direction we'd come from and into the tulles edge. As captain, I'm always around the motor and running the dog off the pods. It just is kind of "my place." The duck hole in the decoy spread was set up in front of us to the south in open water. I'd had Jason put the swan kegs out east, off the bow of the boat, for better visibility from all directions to passing swans. I was going to have to let the swan pass by a bit before there was a safe lane to shoot. Hopefully, it wouldn't set down too early where the vegetation would block a shot. And why didn't I just quick trade places with Jason? I'm clueless. You could hold a square dance down in the boat blind and not be seen when moving. Maybe I was "swan locked." The swan was locked on the glide path, and it was about to happen!

It is funny how time often slows down on events such as this and what you see. I slowly moved my body around, following the bird's glide path to the decoys. Hope was down inside the blind with no visuals, but her head was cocked, listening. Jason's head was just a bump in the rim of the boat blind top. The swan's head was turning back and forth, looking at the plastic trio of three, as its wings ballooned, and it rocked backward to break its progression and speed to the water's surface. It passed into the clear shooting zone, the gun recoiled, and I saw the brake failure. The swan skidded and tumbled across the water. Instantly, it righted itself, and up popped its head. The brass bead of Hope's new gun lined up center high in the neck, and any possible issues of additional efforts of recovery ceased with the gun's report!

A unique memory, and I failed to take a second to better organize the end of it. Out of habit, I called, "Hope!"

From the darkness inside the boat, I could hear claws grabbing metal. I saw the front of the blind move as she found her exit on that end—and then splash! I secured my gun and grabbed the camera. I was excited to say the least! And my photo timing and quality suffered.

Jason had his phone up to get some footage. I don't know how Hope knew where she was going. She came along the inside gunwale of the boat, between it and the vegetation. She was swimming and pushing what looked like a bag of flour toward the back entry of the boat. She couldn't see over the swan or through the wing that was covering her head. She was just pushing it along toward the back pods where she normally worked from.

As I was moving my seat out of the way to get to the pod to take the swan and help Hope in, the commotion started. Hope was hopping into the boat. No swan. She shook inside the boat. Thank you! She started out of the blind the way she came in, but she stopped halfway out. I was finally able to get to the end and observe. She had somehow pushed the swan up onto the pod, climbed up and over it in deep water with no bottom to work from, and was now pulling it by the neck over the lower blind brace and into the boat! Task completed. She shook again and then looked at me like she was asking, "Anything else?"

I just looked at Jason and shook my head. The drive of that forty-eight-pound dog never ceases to amaze me.

We rehashed the hunt, the video, and the photos we had. I lamented the ones I should have had, including an over-the-shoulder shot if I'd been standing where I should have been off that end. Oh, well. We tossed the decoys into the boat in no certain order and putted out to pick up a long-sailing mallard duck Jason had shot earlier. We were breaking a bit of new ice as we went. The sun was touching the western hills as the "boom sha boom" hit plane and headed into the pink fireball. The sound of the ice falling away as we traveled over and through it reminded me that we had been just under Ma Nature's wire. She locked the refuge hard the next day and sent more options south.

So, did I eat the swan? Yes, I did. I fried one breast half straight up just like I do with a lot of puddle ducks. It scored a tad above goldeneye. It was a young swan, which I don't think helped. I put the other half in a crock pot with BBQ sauce, low and slow for eight hours. When I shredded it, it moved up the palate scale to a solid six. I was already beginning my search for the next swan-cooking methodology. I wanted one white mature adult to meet my pellet grill in some marinated fashion. Each bird taken is required to be checked in with the DWR or the feds. This was a Friday night, and they were closed till Monday. I vented (the proper word for removing innards/guts) the swan and let it hang until I could drive back over the hill so they could check it. Then I let it hang an additional four days. I dry-age-hang birds as often as the weather permits. That effort didn't seem to help break the meat down either. I'll try something different on the next one.

BLING! IT IS TIME

I'd watched them on and off through the years loafing around on my neighbor's place out back. I had permission to hunt three small properties behind my house. The geese usually came late in the season and would spend some time loafing around in one of those pastures. There was a great little creek for ducks, and I usually waited for a slow, snowy, warm day to work that. I'd set up along the creek and shoot them as they swung around to go to a roost pond.

I had this weird sympathy for the geese. It might be one of the few places, other than along isolated areas of the river, where they could just hang out that late in the season and not be harassed. This particular year, there seemed to be an overabundance of them. One of the pieces of property had changed hands, and the way its livestock was fed there brought this open swampy area north of it more geese. They would get a drink and then hang out for most of the day. There was just nowhere else good to hide. The geese put themselves far off cover, and it would be like hunting in a parking lot with one exception: snow might help break up my outline.

With what little cover there was from a thin, low weed patch, I added a couple big tumbleweeds and waited for snow. It had been cold and freezing up water without the snow. It finally came. The geese changed their timing just a tad. In a decoy bag, I took three full-bodied decoys, a small folding chair, a closed cell foam pad for Hope, and a bed sheet to cover her. I put on my old army surplus white poncho. My truly enjoyable, "even for cold feet in a blind of my youth" original Sorrel boots, micro loft everything else, including gloves, and off we went. That was it—no layout blind or coffin comfort. If needed, I'd nap sitting up!

Walking out there, I recalled the number of geese my father shot standing by a fence post—and the clobbering my high school buddies and I would give them as we laid on pieces of cardboard under a bed sheet during what we called a "bear laker!" It was the first early blizzard of the year, and if you had a field the geese were using when it came, limits happened quickly! So, we would see how it went. It was truly old school on new-school geese. I would be using the sun at my back and in their eyes. I had the timing down when they showed up. They fed first a quarter mile away, and then they would come get a drink. I wanted to get into the fountain before they arrived at the feed in order to reduce the opportunity for being spotted walking in. Geese have incredible eyesight. The snow patterns on the ground and tumbleweeds couldn't have looked any better. We were doomed for failure! The setup looked too good.

It was twenty-eight degrees, and the sun had been working away to lift the temperature for about thirty minutes. I positioned a sentry and two feeder goose mannequins along the open seep's edge to my left about twenty-five yards. I wanted the sun in their faces and out of their lines of sight. I faced the direction from which they should come, pushing my position as far to the right as I could to open up a good barrel swing in that direction.

Hope was lying on her place to my left and slightly behind me. I tossed the sheet over her, and we waited. The geese were showing up at the feed lot to the north. I think some had already been there, but maybe the snow cover had let me get away with walking in a bit late. Early ducks had already been tempting me. They were big, fat January mallards whose emerald-green heads glistened in the morning sun. Some landed so close I could see their toenails. If we were getting away being undetected by them, maybe we would shoot the geese.

About forty-five minutes into the stakeout, five geese got up and headed our way. The call had stayed in my pocket. There was no need to tell them we were here. They knew where they were going. They were on a rope, barely clearing the fence lines. I'd twisted into the best shooting position the stool and scant cover would allow and mounted the gun to my shoulder to minimize my movement as they closed in. But then they sat down about seventy yards north of us. *What? Dang, I just knew it was too good of a setup to work!*

From the distance of my home, a half mile off, and looking through the spotting scope, maybe I'd misjudged it. No, there was goose sign where I set up. All of a sudden, one of the geese in the bunch began to talk frantically! It marched back and forth on high alert, took to the air, and headed our way. The others followed! It was never three feet above the ground and coming to the decoys. About ten yards from the decoy, I thought the goose was going to land, but it reared back and slammed feetfirst into the plastic sentry decoy, knocking it over and sending it across the ice with all sorts of unnatural sounds that plastic and ice colliding make! I saw Hope's sheet flinch. That lead goose was mad! It honked, flapped, and hissed! It paid no heed to the blob behind the tumbleweed that wasn't there yesterday, and I was about to remove its attitude from the gene pool.

Then the devil showed up. *Go on, ground-pound it. You fooled it. Hell, you shoot turkeys on the ground. Come on, slide that barrel over onto that neck and let 'er rip! Then kill a couple more as they leave.* I fought off the devil! *I just had to stand up, didn't I?*

I stood, and the yakking goose shut up! I was poised like I was going to call "pull" on the skeet range! The goose decided to leave, flying straightaway instead of to the left like it was facing. When it didn't crumple from the first shot, I couldn't believe it! Pretty sure my head was still up and off the stock. The second shot brought it down, but it was still very much alive! A ghost with a black nose was blazing across the ice toward it! Hope shot past two other live geese that were standing right of the decoys about the time she shed the sheet. Live geese! What? Two hadn't left! I guess the commotion had confused them. And I was focused on Mr. or Mrs. Attitude! As Hope piled into the attitude goose, all hell broke loose—and the others decided to leave. They flew toward me and to the right of me. I had one shell and had to wait, wait, wait, for a distance that the pattern would open up. Boom! Two flying became one!

Hope managed the protesting goose back to me where it was promptly laid to rest. It was a huge goose, later weighing in at twelve pounds vented. I pointed across the spring and told Hope to get back! The second goose wasn't as large, and it was dead. The retrieve had a little more organization and class about it. I was standing still, and Hope was about halfway back with the goose. The three amigos were still minus their plastic leader when I heard a quiet honk behind me. *Crap. That was close, and the gun is empty.*

I dug quickly in my coat pocket for a round, dropped it in the chamber, and slammed the action shut. I turned to my left and watched a lone goose flare off of what were now the two amigos and a bed sheet. Hope showed up with goose number two, and then she left to get the new arrival I'd just piled up. *Holy cow. That was crazy and fast!*

"Come on, Hope. Let's get gathered up and out of here so not to wreck it so we can have some other days." Yeah, I was talking to the dog! Don't you?

I was tying the baling twine around the geese so I could drag them when I first noticed a band! A freaking band! All the waterfowl over the years, and this was my first banded bird! Bonus! And more mystery to unwind. I can't wait to call it in. Goose number two had been the ringbearer.

And so it went for about a month out the back forty. We'd slide in, pick off a few, and then get out. The past two years, the weather has been different. The feed stayed the same, but the water changed—and so did the geese in any number. I've been content to watch the few there were with the spotting scope. I'm not sure how I'll have a year better than that year out there again anyway. It was just kind of magical. Bling! As for Hope and her opinion, she just goes with the flow. No muss, no fuss. She is just happy to go along in ghost costumes or whatever. It makes me wonder what the world would be like if everyone got along so well.

Chapter 19

COVE AND COMPANY

I'M TAKING A BREAK FROM the Hope's short stories to introduce you to another influential dog. Cove is part of my nephew and niece's family. To understand Cove, you need to understand her human partners. I'm not sure I understand them, well, at least one of them. Denton is my brother's oldest son. Being first in line, he automatically was exposed to hunting and was completely "ate up" with it.

Cove is the first dog that was Denton's total responsibility and part of his new family. Kelsie, Denton's wife, has a mild heart condition. Cove is out of Kelsie's family dogs. Cove can alert the condition coming on. Kelsie has great training abilities with animals. She was working on Cove to be a clown, and Denton was working on Cove to be a huntress. They were both attending Utah State University, and Cove got to live with them on campus because of her service provision. We would see them frequently.

I could see this little confusion with Cove's handling starting to rise. I did not want to be a complete "Uncle Butt-In," but I was gaining a large amount of sympathy for Cove. I worked to monitor the training into a compatible bliss influencing when I could. Once you got past the "wired factor" of Cove, you could see she is extremely smart and full of drive. When the black Lab purists would see pictures of her and Hope riding on the boat, I'd get all sorts of farm talk hassle. They called her a Holstein— and it got worse from there. You see, Cove was a springer spaniel, and a spring, she was! Denton had a Lab named Maxi that was trained about to the level of Coke. They both served a purpose with Riley and Denton growing up with a field dog. Neither lad did much of the specific training other than to take the dogs into the field.

My chance to truly influence the training of Cove came when they ask us if we'd watch her while they went to some university training/ competition for Denton's agricultural vocational studies. My goal was to teach this "water in hot grease" pooch to "place." She wouldn't be able to spend time in the boat without that. It's a safety issue first. And she was wired, wired, wired, wired—that is four wireds! Not your typical three. I had about a day to pull this off. I got a bit of help from Hope since the word "place" really was one of her favorite words.

When they came to pick up Cove, she was all a wiggle as only this springer could be. She greeted them as they came in by spinning circles and doing half somersaults. I think they loved this dog more than they did each other. In the middle of the "so glad to see you," I said, "Cove, place!" She stopped the greeting cold and went over and got on her new place. That brought an immediate halt to the room, and I was able to talk with them both about consistency in training and how it was OK to teach tricks—and how to get feathers too—but there had to be lines, parameters, and consistency to help the dog understand.

I grew extremely fond of this little dog, and I looked forward to seeing her as much as I did them in a different kind of anticipation. I did take some liberty to lightly chew on my nephew as best I could allow myself about hunting her differently when it was cold. She has a pretty tight coat, but it is more akin to Hope's light coat. Cove's coat will get length to it, and it does have a tighter/thicker base. I'm always concerned about a dog's comfort in the cold. He eventually told me he'd added a vest to the gear list.

Cove wasn't a big fan of the boat blind. She couldn't see out of it, and that drove her batty. The first time we tore into a flock of ducks when she was along, and she heard them slapping the water, she broke place and banged around off the mesh lining walls like a ping-pong ball. Over time, she worked a hole loose next to her place that she could lay with her head out and watch. Hope was always happy when I let her out on the pod and then give her a line. It didn't take long for Cove to learn the stairway back into the boat. One swim around the boat to the pod, and she had it down the next time.

This little dog has pulled numerous birds from the local waters. The variety of water challenges continued to help her be better. She now hunts the upper Snake River where they now reside. And she is in it till the ice floes chase her off. Her "get it done" drive rivals and exceeds many of the pure "water dogs" I've hunted around. Cove has a sister named Sky.

Sky lives at my brother's house. She is a dual blue-eyed dog. There is an old saying about never trusting a blue-eyed dog. Sky is supposed to be my niece's responsibility, but for the most part, she has captured my brother's focus. She was raised with my other nephew's Lab, Roxy. Roxy has been a dog that I will call a "take-it-over" kind of dog. Cove and Sky race to the dummy, and it ends up, well, messy. Roxy usually wins.

Roxy is coming in to her own as a water dog. When they take Sky and Roxy hunting, Sky is happy to just be there and doesn't participate. What happened in the yard with bumpers is reflected in the field. Sky was labeled a "this dog won't hunt" yard dog. The blue eyes against the black-and-white hide have this mystic look about them. In a way, it's almost haunting. I'm always teasing them about never trusting a blue-eyed dog. She proved her label away this past season.

Roxy had puppies, and there were four hunters who were going to be out of dog power on opening day. They were going to hunt a farm pond. It is a big pond surrounded by a wall of cattails. It can be a challenge to a seasoned dog. If you are young with long legs and watch your shots, you can wade to the duck when shot. Most places, you sink to your knees, and it is a workout. For want of any other options, they took Sky and expected little from her other than a muddy coat full of burs. Seventeen retrieves later, Sky had earned her water dog pin! You never know until they go— and it is true about a blue-eyed dog!

Chapter 20

A HIGHER POWER

ROXY'S PARTNER IS DENTON'S YOUNGER brother, Huston. We call him Hoot for short. Being behind Denton and an older sister, and then a sister behind him in age—the baby of the family—put Hoot in what I will call the observation seat while growing up.

Hoot spends a bunch of time watching and listening. I'm not sure why I noticed it, but I did. With all the hunting options provided to him, he tilted a tad heavier toward waterfowling organically. Denton had blazed a bit of a trail by chasing everything, but Roxy was Hoot's idea. Maybe he reminded me of me.

Hoot put in for a Utah swan tag as a nonresident and drew his first year at age seventeen. They set a few tags aside from the general draw to improve the youth draw odds. Nonresident youth have good odds at drawing. Riley had drawn again the prior year, and he and Denton mutinied my boat and got that accomplished for Riley with his first swan. Denton can't seem to draw.

I picked up a bonus point that year, and Hoot and I drew this year. The phone conversation was after the drawing. The negotiation went something like this: "When can you take me?" I calendared a range of days. Hoot lives a three-hour drive from my home. He has a great buddy he wanted to bring along for the duck hunting, but I felt like, in this case, three might be a crowd. I hated to have a youth stay home, but we were short on days and long on odds. Hoot would have to put up with the "old unc" alone. We only had a couple days to pull it off, and the birds had not yet showed up in force. And I'm really a newbie at swan hunting as far as my waterfowling history goes. I needed to luck it up, and reducing some management challenges would help.

STOP: PUBLIC SERVICE ANNOUNCEMENT!

It is March 21, 2020. It's Saturday at 5:45 a.m. Thirty-two degrees. I've just scanned the news coverage of the coronavirus again. I've told those who know of my first attempt to write a full-blown book that it may be a book that is never published. In that case, at least it is a fleshed-out part of my journals for any interest in who Grandpa or Great-Grandpa was.

I take news coverage with large grains of salt. I scan through it for common threads of reality. My college studies, years ago, were in and around the journalism students as part of my postgraduate work in organizational communications. The internet was not yet available with its instant ability to quickly spew useless garbage or valuable information. We programmed punch cards back in those days. I didn't choose computer science as a field of study, but one phrase has always remained with me: "Garbage in, garbage out!" That is Computer Science 101.

Behind every computer effort is a human carrying a collective bag of experiences. The applications that spew information are driven by the "truth" of math in the form of an algorithm. Here is the truth: Algorithms can only be set to adjust to what we know for sure, based on the information available at the time of programming. Computers cannot think or adapt on their own to a change in a given situation. They need to be reprogrammed. What is a "smart" phone? If I don't manipulate mine, it just lays there looking at me. Sometimes it will ring and ping. Other than that, it is pretty useless if I don't pick it up.

One of the stronger discussions of my college life was with a fairly new doctorate-seeking assistant professor who taught a journalism ethics course. In my final paper, I scribbled way outside the lines because we were told that was acceptable to do. My effort ended up involving my advisor and the college dean, and I'm pretty sure it knocked on the door of the provost. It was difficult to get the grade change, but it happened. It is difficult for things to be absolute.

"We want you to think way beyond the realms of possibility and express it!"

Honestly, I don't even remember the topic, but I expressed it contrary to her personal algorithm.

"No, that is too far past the realm I directed!"

There really wasn't a right or wrong answer—just a couple of folks toting around bags. I don't recall "bad manners" being justified or protected in free speech, but they are not without consequence either. The news briefings are so socially wrong, piled up with disrespect to one another, and it is hard to see where it starts—let alone if it will ever end. If COVID-19 doesn't teach us anything else, it may teach us how working to get along with one another can be a painful but honorable effort.

It is now April 21, 2020, and I'm on my second proof of this writing. It took just shy of a month for social discord to elevate due to the virus shutdown. Being out of work for many people is a tough spot. I'm there at this moment, thanks to the virus, but my situation may be easier than many of those storming the Capitol steps. I get the frustration when those "people" above you who control things don't seem to listen—let alone relate.

I hadn't established an "essential position" since being laid off after twenty-one years in the outdoor industry prior to COVID-19 coming along. The part-time shuttle bus driving position I scrambled into went with the college closure due to the virus. I now wonder why being sixty years old couldn't be classified as essential. The young leadership of the tanked corporation I spent my last two years with after the private brand I worked for was purchased just needed to ask me, and I would have told them how to solve their PR issue. I'd still be there. Their stock prices would be up. And you would still get this book. It may take a tad longer to get it written. But we/they/us are driven by the "bean," and balancing it, in fairness to all, takes a lot of effort.

There is always a cause and effect. And you can't get water from a rock. Those statements are truths. I'm encouraged by those willing to overlook those who may owe them in kind of a reverse "pay it forward" during this pandemic. I have never eaten at a Shake Shack, but I was encouraged by their DNA that they gave money back from the small business stimulus because others needed it more! And what have we learned about the ecology of our planet during this challenging time? Water is clearer, air is cleaner, and Ma Nature has a chance to take a breath! What will we apply as we move back toward the life we have known in the event we can get a handle on this nasty germ? Will we change a bad habit that negatively affects others? If big bank behavior is any sign, get a mason jar and a shovel!

People are tired of being in the house. I'm tired of it. My boat opens up some options for me. Northern Utah does not have a mandatory stay-at-home order yet. On Saturday, the local launch onto "the pond" was a zoo. It is a small launch, and in a normal year, at this time of year, the parking lot is mostly vacant. The virus says this isn't a normal year. All the vehicles that were transporting canoes to motorboats didn't display the Quagra Muscle paperwork on the dashboard.

Most nonmotorized boaters I've talked with down there over the past few years have no clue about what that is about—even though there are two large display boards with explanations and requirements posted on them. Cause and effect—let us not create another negative out of a negative, shall we? This little bugger can jam up our irrigation systems, electrical production, and possibly move upstream to culinary water.

Read intently the next few paragraphs—and then think about your relationship with your dog. If you/we can't get it right with the consistent loyalty desire that dogs truly want to be involved in, how are you/we going to get it right with each other?

If you are reading this in book form, then I guess we got through the virus thing—and I was lucky enough to find someone to risk helping this to market. This writing has become part of my contribution to positive social change. Give the dog an open avenue for "*try.*" We all need to try to do the best we can with what we have available. There are a bunch of what-ifs and maybe-ifs in the paths of life. If we make mistakes, as humans, we can work to understand the failures—and then apologize and work to make it right if we have hurt someone or something.

Ask for help from your power sources, things, and others around you to help you become a better player in life. That can help you contribute positively to the space you take up on earth. I have found, as I have moved along through life, sometimes staying out of the way looks to be a weakness, but it really can be a strength. The contribution may be as small as your place in the boat for safety contributions toward stability and staying afloat.

Most of my passengers who float in my boat ask what they can do to help. And while, "Sit here" and "Move there" might not seem like much, they are what is needed at the time. Maybe you will have to partake in what the old-timers call the "hair of the dog that bit you" in order to get moving on a forward path. I've mostly heard that phrase used in reference to folks wanting to change the outcome of what started out as a happy journey with a little alcohol and just enough to "take the edge off." And then it went south in a hurry to what we now know to be a condition brought on by genetics. I don't think "I apologize," "I'm truly sorry," and "Thank you" are genetically controlled statements. They can be learned, but the "hair of the dog" can help you acquire the sincerity that is meaningful and creates good results.

I've made the statement a few times in this writing that certain things are a mystery to me. My general given nature is to understand and resolve challenges given to me and others that create discomfort and devalue existence. That pathway to a solution is often taxed with frustration and discomfort, but I am glad the mysteries are there to continue to be considered. This may be one of the reasons I like waterfowling and hunting in general—because of the continual change and the effort you give to figure it out to the extent Ma Nature will allow.

That is why I don't own a trail camera for my big game hunting, which can help rob me of the mystery. While video monitoring can be useful for conservation efforts, such as discovering the negative effects of ravens on sage hen nests. (Yes, really. Who'd have thought?) With all my hard pounding on my former classmates who chose to be purist journalists and fight their political leanings every day, I continue to appreciate that they are there swinging with their "bags of experiences." Once in a while, there is a statement that rings with honesty. Your dog is always honest. Spend some time observing it and hearing the whispers.

In an interview the other day about the coronavirus, one journalist said, "I have a buddy in the green business. He deals with Mother Nature all the time and has told me that she will let you do this and that, but in the end, she does what she wants—when she wants. She always bats last and bats one thousand."

I hope we weather the virus and each other. The dog, Hope, most likely hopes we weather it. She senses something is off, and it's not just the yellow dog with the black tail named Ruby in her space. Ruby was supposed to be black and small, like Hope, and be named Faith. That was the plan, but plans change. The full story may be at the end of this writing. For now, we will explore the word "faith" as it pertains to swans, the virus, and a positive future.

Lots of experts, referring to the virus, are saying, "I have faith; we will get through this." So, what is faith? Who thought up the description and application? Working to uncover the when and why could lead you toward an unsolvable mystery. And there is the possibility that you'd just go nuts. The word "faith," as I know it, can be used to describe groups; "They are of the Baptist faith." If you're a person who buys into Christianity, then you can find pretty good examples in the Bible of how the word faith is used. If you're an atheist, then maybe you applied the word to something because of habitual hearing. What if you are Buddhist, Druid, Muslim, or any other applied title east or west of Christianity? Here is a definition of the word faith that I have grown up around. It can make you feel a bit like a gerbil on a wheel—and it is within the context of a religious use.

"Faith is not to have a perfect knowledge of things. Therefore, if you have faith, you hope for things which are not seen which are true." You can thank an ancient author for those words. The definition itself requires you to participate in the activity of faith. I know it may hurt your head. For the record, I lean hard toward the "faith" of a higher power. My "oh, ye of little faith" side is still working to sort out just what exactly that "power" is and/or what it looks like, but if I knew, I wouldn't have to have "faith," right? Isn't it great? A mystery to be considered for the slow moments in the boat! Yes, pass the aspirin, hair of the dog, dontchu know? Thank you, Hollywood and *Fargo*. Rant complete. Thank you.

Hoot had more faith in me than he most likely should have had. I was ready to pull out when he arrived, and we headed to the launch as fast as the hour-long drive would allow! There was one rig there ahead of us. We dropped in the boat, and Hope jumped to her place on the bow. I fired the motor, slammed the throttle, and zipped toward the point. The one boat ahead of us concerned me. *Please, don't let them be there.* The other boat wasn't on the point, but they were close enough that if I'd have set up right where I wanted to, I was going to encroach on them. There is an unwritten ethic locally: While waterfowling, be at least two hundred yards off of other hunters' setups. Yes, I would be outside that limit, but it was still too close for me. So, we slid to the north toward a walk-in dike. Ugh! We split the distance and called it good. We were still in the flight path, but the dike was concerning.

We shot a couple ducks, and while geese don't really like this area, I clobbered a hog of a honker. Hope got to practice moving mass back to the boat. It was now swan thirty, and we had to lay off the ducks. The dike walkers started to show up. A couple of high groups of swans were on the move. I think our absence of a full swan spread kept the dike walkers from positioning themselves to suck off our decoys. Across the bay, half a mile away, were two big spreads of white plastic—and they were not pulling down anything either.

Fifteen minutes before time ended, seven swans made it past the dike and slid down the flight line. Some duck hunters had showed up on the point south of us where I'd shot my first swan and where I wanted to be today, but we moved because of the other hunters who were in the area earlier. They had just shot at some ducks, and that put these white birds on the think! They gave us a look and made a big swing back past, and I almost called the shot. They were pushing the edge of pellet power to the outside—not the inside—so I let them swing again, but they didn't. We gathered up the decoys, swung out, and used the boat to retrieve a long-sailing greenhead mallard duck. We putted back to the launch, thinking and observing. It just didn't look nor feel good.

On the ride home, we were discussing options. The birds just were not there in numbers, it seemed. Hoot had one full day ahead to hunt, and the weather didn't look to cooperate to help move birds during the day. I knew one other place to look about a half-hour drive south of where we were. I tossed out the option of an all-day event starting at 4:00 a.m. from the house till shooting time ended the next day to explore the sight. Option 2 was getting here earlier for the evening flight and setting up farther south, closer to the point, before the evening crowd could take it. He took option 2, and this set us up for success. The old boy was pretty thankful he selected option 2 for all the reasons. Going to the first option would be a total crapshoot. At least here, we had seen a few swans in flight. Not to mention he was tired—and so was I.

We were motoring toward the point by 2:00 p.m. The parking lot was vacant when we arrived. There were, however, two big spreads of white plastic about half a mile across the bay from us against the east bank—again. I was pretty sure they had come downriver that morning and were committed to the day. We eased around the point and then turned west into the first east-and-west-running open water lane. I set the boat against a small island with the bow facing east. Twenty yards east of us was open water clear to the east bank. To the west of us one hundred yards, little islands started to eat up open water. There was a lane coming into us from the south. Behind the island, we rested against was an open area that was large enough to accommodate a group of swans landing. It was kind of a "flip the coin" deal. I asked Hope what she thought and didn't get much feedback other than a tail wag. That is pretty much an "I'll deal with what comes my way." Hope was just glad to be there. Her response is always honest.

We spread eighteen duck blocks around as if they had been loafing most of the day. We were careful not to block any runways. At the east end of the entrance, we put the swan decoys for visibility and a lead-in to the runway. We threw up the boat blind and hunkered in. The weather was warm and calm, and the afternoon dragged on. Nothing moved till three thirty when the first boat for the evening hunts came out. I hoped our location would also discourage other hunters' abilities to crowd us. So far, that was a win.

At about four o'clock, a small flock of pesky gadwalls showed up. They were the result of other boats getting back into setup. With nothing else in sight, we decide a little warm-up was called for. Hope was thankful to swim, and then the air really died. I mean, it was heavy and calm. There was now shooting in the distance.

An hour off of closing time, I texted my wife and told her that it was brutal. We had yet to even see a high-flying swan at a distance. I was getting really antsy. I zipped my phone away and looked down at Hope. She had crashed out and was offering no help. I really wanted Hoot to get a chance at a swan. I second-guessed not calling the shot last night and then ended up with a pleading negotiation with the higher power. And in the middle of it, Hoot said, "Here come some swans!" My head popped up through my portal in the top of the blind like a dysfunctional jack-in-the-box. I almost pulled every muscle in my neck trying to slow down. I didn't know how close "here comes" meant.

They were south of us maybe a quarter mile but on line. At half the distance, they were losing altitude. They eased a tad to the east and were on the glide. Not quite yet committed—but looking to be. At 150 yards, they swung a bit of a right and lit. Yeah, go figure. I have no clue why they wouldn't have finished. I whispered to Hoot that maybe they would swim over and to keep an eye on them.

Hoot could sit, and his eyes were just across the top of the blind. I had to strain upright because I'd grabbed the wrong chair yesterday and didn't get it changed out. Five minutes went by, and they showed no signs of swimming our way. Hope was up. She had heard them calling and felt our movements. I looked at her and shook my head. Her tail moved slowly from side to side with minimal enthusiasm.

I peeked again. Maybe they had moved a bit closer. I checked my watch. Forty-five minutes left. There was still no meaningful shooting in the distance. It was deader than last night. If anything could be described as flat, this was it! I tapped on the door. "So, uh, God? I don't really need to kill another swan today. Yeah, I know I said I'd like a big mature adult, and then I may stop hunting them because, really, they just don't eat that well. And so it may look like I'm asking for me, but I'm really not. I'm sure you know that, sorry. This kid is running out of time, and we could use a little help here, so I'm asking."

I didn't even have a suggestion for him. Mentally, I was worn out. I scratched Hope's head, and then I felt a gust of wind. I don't mean a puff either! It moved the boat. And it built and built until there were whitecaps, and there wasn't a cloud in the sky. The swans had quieted, and now they were really talking. I told Hoot they were about to get up. "They are going to get right up into that NE wind and be gone!"

And that is what they did!

I looked down at Hope and cussed under my breath.

Hoot hissed, "They are coming this way!"

"What?"

He asked if he should shoot about the time my eyes cleared the hole's edge as I peeked to see. The wind had pushed them, and they were right in the wheelhouse.

"Shoot 'em!" I hollered.

Bang, bang, bang!

Oh, crap. He's empty and missed! I swung up on the last bird, and I gave it the wet-rag complex.

On hearing the splashdown, Hope dove past me and onto the boat pod.

I said, "Stay!" I wanted to make sure it was dead.

In a frantic voice, Hoot said, "They are coming back!"

I traded my gaze from the flopping swan on the water and looked west. Sure enough, here they came back.

"I'm jammed up!" Hoot muttered. I could hear him jacking and slamming the action around!

"Here, take mine. It's on safety—one in the spout and one in the magazine!" I could hear they were close but didn't dare look.

Hoot said, "I'm good!"

The swans swung to the north as they approached my end of the boat. I dropped down in the blind hole as they did. When they had cleared me, Hoot touched off the first round. No joy! Then the second round, nothing folded! Oh, no. Please! Bang! The last swan fell over the back side of the island! Did this just happen? Well, thank you, God!

I told Hoot to get out of the boat and wade around the island. I would knock the boat blind down and get it ready to go. If the bird was alive and out of range, we could chase it down. Hoot bailed off the front of the bow a bit like Hope would—just not nearly as gracefully. He was excited, and I was excited. No, hell, I was a mess! I glanced toward the swan I'd shot now hung up against the reeds about forty yards away. Hope was looking at it too, and I sent her and continued to organize the boat. I looked up when I heard Hope on the pod. Then it dawned on me that I hadn't taken any photos or videos!

I grabbed the swan by the neck and pulled it—and Hope—into the boat. It was huge, noticeably larger than my first one.

Hoot hollered, "Here it is. It's dead!"

In a couple minutes, Hoot showed up all grins with another mature swan.

We took some photos and picked up the decoys, and with about ten minutes left in the season, we headed toward the launch. I noticed that the wind had laid down. It was glass! And another odd thing was that the wind mostly blows, when it does over there, in this order: out of the northwest, west, north, south, east, and rarely from the east. Never have I known it to blow from the northeast.

When I tell the story to the locals who know swans and really know the refuge, I just get a long blank stare, and then they say, "You've got to be kidding me!"

"Nope. With Hope as my witness, I swear it!"

Hoot pulled the trailer, boat, Hope, and me up from the launch and into the parking lot. We stowed items away for the hour-long drive home and listened to the cry of the night that truly only waterfowlers understand and appreciate fully. The sky was full of birds, and the swans had arrived by the hundreds. Go figure! Oh, *me* of little faith.

Chapter 21

FAITH? NO RUBY!

"**N**O, YOU SHOULDN'T GET A dog. You are not in a position for a dog. I don't care if the grand-girls are asking or not. They have a dog. They can come and play with Hope anytime they want to!" Seems like I'd had this similar discussion many years back over what became our house rat, Maggie. Josie, JP for short, is our daughter. We named after the movie character Josie Wales. I know—what were we thinking?) She is as bullheaded as her mother. And while female, she really has that Clint Eastwood thing about her. You know that thing just before the gun comes out with the offer to "go ahead and make my day."

Their yard was fenced, but it was not dog-proofed on the back side as well as it needed to be. Where they lived, the dogs had to be in the house at night. Both she and her husband worked. All three of her girls had grown up around Hope. The oldest granddaughter was four when she started running Hope to bumpers. Hope is the patient pillow that will do anything for them for a bit of attention. But this one would come as a puppy and all that which comes with it.

They brought both puppies by for me to see them. No, they gained no favor with me, the pups, or the potential owners. They decided to take the yellow one with the black-tipped tail. A couple days later, they asked if the girl could drop off the puppy at my house—and they would come get it when they were off work. *Grrr!* "I guess."

I took the pup from the gal, and she drove away. Fifty dollars included all the shots. At least the price was right? I held the little gal up and looked her in the eye. I said, "I think we are going to see more of each other than either one of us will like!" She was asleep on my lap when they came to get her and my extra pet porter. A yellow Lab with half a black tail? What is up with that? Maybe she'd grow out of it. Not my dog. I told them I'd teach them how to teach sit, stay, and come for the sake of the pup.

Training the parents was more difficult than training the pup. My oldest granddaughter had a better grip on it than her parents could get. I often wondered if I shouldn't work on some kind of a bill to introduce to law about the humanity of putting dog "owners" down or be rescued if they cannot be trained to train. (I'm kidding, OK? Kind of.)

When Ruby was five months old, she was working to rescue herself. I had dog-proofed the yard as best as I could, but Ruby would find a way out, usually in the hardest way available. It was like she was saying, "Let's get right to the hard stuff." I'd suggested not leaving her to roam in the house and yard if no one was around. I could sense enough anxiety in her that I could see her eating a hole through the wall and escaping outside after trashing the inside. There was a lockable dog door, which I think would have made matters worse if she was left to roam inside the house. Locking her outside just gave her time to figure out an escape plan from the yard.

I was able to spend enough time with the pooch when they would come to visit that she was getting the basics, including retrieving. She wouldn't load in the back of their car unless they picked her up. That took me ten minutes to teach. I had put off looking for another pup to replace Hope as she aged because I just had this funny feeling about Ruby. Yes, Ruby. Where did they come up with that name anyway? Sounds like what you'd name a milk cow. Then it happened. I went into the salon to get a haircut from my daughter, and she told me that Ruby had run away!

Inside, I just blew up! I looked her straight in the eyes and said, "Sorry, I don't know how to help you." I was swallowing the "I told you so" as fast as I could gobble it back down. We discussed the find-the-dog options. I told her I was out on the search. It was just too much to do. Yes and no, I could see her countenance fall. Since I fought off the "I told you so," it was the best way I could administer painful growth. And, yes, it is contrary to my solutional nature of the path of least resistance. Parenting—I need to get over it. Grandparenting is much easier.

When I left the salon, I drove to the rescue center to get educated about what you did to find a dog nowadays if it ends up in the system. It was on the way home anyway—if you figured it in a loop. Finishing the loop on the way home, I decided to drive past my daughter's place and see if Ruby had come home by chance.

As I pulled into the neighborhood, I met the animal control officer, and I flagged him down. I asked if he had seen a yellow pup with the stupid-looking black tail. He said that he had gotten word that it had been reported missing, and he came to the area to look. He saw the pup following him up the road as he drove to the house. She went up and sat on the porch as my daughter arrived at the house.

I drove to the house, pulled into the drive, got out of the car, and said, "You are lucky." I opened the back hatch, called to Ruby, and told her to get in. "I will keep her at the house until we can figure this out." I headed for home. I was relieved the dog was OK, relieved it didn't turn into a bigger mess, and aggravated that I was about to house a yellow dog—whose name was not Faith!

Chapter 22

FAITH BECAUSE OF RUBY

ABOUT THE ONLY THING IN life that is predictable is that life isn't predictable! And that water from a rock thing. Who would have thought that the next world war would be a stinking virus? There will be plenty of folks writing books about it. This project was started long before it revealed itself, and it may very well change the course of this effort. I've worked to keep it focused on the dogs and the teachers that they are.

It is March 25, 2020. It snowed a skiff here in the Cache Valley. I have had my update to the COVID-19 predicament via Fox News and MSNBC. I did a bit of correction to this document and then went out to feed Hope and Ruby. There is just an eerie stillness about the calm outside. A month ago, Wednesday traffic on state Highway 91 from Preston, Idaho, which is seventeen miles north of Smithfield, Utah, would have been more crowded. The traffic has continued to lie down since the suggestion of social distancing. Most likely, there still isn't enough compliance to the federally suggested strategy of only essential workers working. We are about seven days away from seeing if that has had any positive effects. Our state health department in Utah strongly suggested yesterday that medical procedures that could be put off along with dental work and vet visits would help with the shortages of masks and gowns that are needed for front-line health workers dealing with the crisis. The experts "hope" that the coming warmer weather will also help lay down this mess. And they have "faith" that we will get through it—as do I. Not sure how we may look as a society, or act, or if I'll even be around to observe it. By definition, my wife and I are in the higher-risk zone. I may be on the "less than a dog" scale instead of the "couple more" I'd gauged my existence by.

Both of the dogs followed me into the house today. Ruby needs her ears cleaned, and Hope's bouncing on her legs backward past the kennel gate. Hope gives me this "Please rescue me from that yellow thing" sign language, which has been difficult to overlook lately. They are both laying on their places where they can keep an eye on me. They both wore out their welcomes with Mom by rousting her out of bed. What does she expect? She has spoiled them on the mornings they are indoors with a fried egg.

I've always worried about crowding anything, especially people, into a large pile. It just isn't healthy or helpful. I was lucky and grew up where I had space handy. We seem to be on this accelerated growth kick as a nation and a world. There is usually too much speed and not enough thought put into the effort.

This valley I live in—and, yeah, I'm a hypocrite because I'm here—just wants to gobble up every piece of land available and stick a structure on it. If it's wet, drain it! If it's hay, curb and gutter. Who needs milk and beef anyway? I was discussing our plight with a member of the county council recently. He is a landowner, and his comment kind of surprised me: "How you going to stop it?"

My simple answer was this: "Can the building permit onslaught."

A township across the river from us pulls water from a well a quarter of a mile west of my house. They stepped in and got a moratorium on septic systems in and around our area to protect that well. Right after that, a developer slick-Willy'd the property immediately west of me and popped up three homes with septic systems and stuck them on one well. He owns the well and charges a use fee to those he sold the homes to. What? But he will make it up to open spaces and any scarring to the wetlands by planting some trees somewhere. What? It changed the whole natural drain system, and the county had to come in and fix it. I'm pretty sure the developer didn't get charged a dime.

What the township next to us did with the septic order was to ensure some type of wetlands activity in a geographical distance of the well. I like to kid folks when these issues come up in conversation using our closed Kmart in the valley. It has been vacant for several years. "Did you hear what they are going to do with the Kmart?" I ask.

"No, what?" is the reply.

And they are leaning in listening intently when I tell them. "They are going to knock it down, plow the parking lot, and plant corn!" I say as pie-faced as I can muster.

This gets me the tipped-head look that Ruby often gives me but deeper in concern, with wrinkled brows. Ninety percent of them ask, "Why would they do that?"

The answer is, "They wouldn't do that." At least we are talking and thinking.

I'm a mile out of town in the county, and the small city of Smithfield just southeast of us can't seem to wait to annex, annex, annex. Annexation does nothing but build a false sugar-high tax base that creates sustainability issues down the road. Most public service systems are overburdened, and no one wants to pay more taxes to have them sustained. Cities would sooner dump noncompliant wastewater into our Bear River and pay a fine than bring it to compliance with taxation on wastewater service. It is about the cost savings. Dump it in the river—out of sight, out of mind. Then, as in our case, the valley citizens go swimming in it because, well … all water is created equal to them. The Bear River Bird Refuge (Google it) is the remaining filter before the water gets to the Great Salt Lake's fresh and saltwater causeway systems. The separations each have a unique purpose. Then there is the evaporation and lake effect snow building that deposits moisture and whatever else is in it into the snowpack and runoff above the Wasatch Front. Some of whatever mysteries that are left in that moisture, good and bad, get filtered out for drinking uses along the Wasatch Front. The Bear River water system that Ma Earth built in this region, headwaters in the Uintah Mountains east of the Wasatch front, is ultimately all connected. Being with dogs in the outdoors brought these things to my attention.

My dogs have helped me learn about conservation from more than the superficial surfaces that are exposed by the info usually disseminated to Joe Q. Public's casual, if at all, observance. They force me to get out and into the environment and pay attention. While I'm not an environmental scientist, I do notice change and question what I see. Moss growing on the boat launch with a water temp of 38–42 degrees after ice out just isn't normal, and it's been building earlier over the past five years during very different weather years. By May, you will have difficulty standing up on the launch due to the moss. And the moss remains longer into the year. It isn't just the slipping on ice I watch for now on mid-October mornings when I launch the boat. So, Ruby should keep me in the field solidly for a few more years to see the wonders of nature along with the challenges thereof. Ma Nature and the specifics of COVID-19 may have something to say about the length of my participation.

Chapter 23

LEANING INTO IT

URING RUBY'S TRAINING, I NOTICE her posture when she waits for the retrieval signal. She leans forward. She sometimes leans so far forward that I think she will tip onto her nose. Her relief comes from stating her name or the word *back*! Then, like a sprinter out of the blocks, she digs for ground. Coke had go. Hope had go, go. This pooch has go, go, go!

Sometimes Ruby's speed gets her overshooting the mark. She always works it out, but it can take a bit of time. Hope, on the other hand, because of experience and age, just works through it at a slower, methodical pace. She continues to use her strongest sense, which is her nose. It's almost as if she checks the wind before she starts into it, especially if the find isn't obvious and immediately visible to sight.

The two of them remind me a lot of my journey in and around the politics of hunting. They also confirm the movement(s) of others who I have used as mentors ahead of me in those efforts. Oftentimes, I will restrict Ruby to observing Hope and then allow her to have a go at whatever I'm trying to teach her. It is amazing to watch the learning curve reduce. As far as physical efforts and the challenges brought to outdoor sporting dogs, in my experiences, ages three through nine are money. So, that is seven years of working in the field when things work well. The first two years are spent with them and me adjusting to one other. Their last few years are dependent on me to notice what accommodations need to be made for them as it pertains to their physical efforts.

With Hope and Coke, there was a visible changing of the guard. While Coke was happy to dig them out and into the air, she became perfectly happy with watching Hope gather them up and bring them to hand.

I should see that change this year with Ruby and Hope. Last year, it was on the edge. It was a tough year for waterfowling last year. I got lucky a few days before Christmas, and things lined up well. I had both dogs on the river. The flows were good for an old dog and new dog, and well … I just have difficulty leaving one home. I was torn between the new dog getting experience and the old dog having a good time. So I will just let it happen and see what rolls out.

Hope owns this section of river, and she knows when we are headed there just by the gear I take. The anticipation whining starts about seven miles from the spot. The birds were there, so I didn't even take the decoys from the rig. I was working to drop the ducks where retrieves were conducive for all. It happened and went fast. When Ruby loped to a downed bird, Hope was not the nine-year-old she was but transformed into the five-year-old rocket of her prime. Ruby was able to gather up one bird while Hope was busy in the river. The last bird of the day was falling toward land about fifteen yards from the blind. Out of the corner of my eye, I could see Hope positioning for it like a shortstop on a pop fly. Ruby was out and alongside her but wasn't looking up. She had left the blind because Hope had and I'd allowed it. The duck hit the ground in front of Hope, and she had it on the first bounce and was back in the blind before Ruby even knew what had happened.

I'm in that ninth year and/or inning with the politics of wildlife and conservation issues. I often wonder who is left to lean into it. I'm concerned about the mentors. Who are they and what are they representing? Do they even know what to represent? And more importantly, is that representation for all the right reasons? It is yet to be seen what will transpire from this virus mess. I am trying to look for the positive, as I'm sure many of you did/have. (I say did/have exercising hope and faith.) One positive is that we will be able to see more clearly who and what we as a society have become. And more so what we value. In my early forties, I was taught by a borderline antihunter who represented a predator protection group here in Utah the importance of the words *intrinsic values*. I was serving on a regional advisory council (RAC) as a sportsman's representative. Our assignment was to gather public input on wildlife and conservation issues. Then we were to put our findings forward in some reasonable order to the Wildlife Board, who would then construct any policy changes coupled with the biologists' inputs.

We were taking input on cougar hunting. This individual explained that there are people who will never see a cougar in the wild. The thought that they might was an intrinsic value to them. It rang pretty true with me. It is why I do what I do in the outdoors. So those folks really are not any different than I am under each our skins. It starts to get crazy and out of focus when we get selfish and remove the *work through it* effort.

Over the years, while serving on various wildlife committees that had to do with policy changes, I have developed a question I like to toss in the foray about the time all the selfishness is laid on the table. The question needs a foundation. "What in this pile of opinions, laced with some biology, is actually good for the wildlife we are discussing?" We really need to sort it into priority piles based on the goal before we can identify the best answer or answers. It doesn't matter if you want it as a human this way or that. The question is simply "Is it good for wildlife?" You see, some people don't value wildlife intrinsically, or any other way for that matter. And some folks, for all their good intentions, just run over nature and not necessarily on purpose. It will be interesting to see what we learn other than a windfall of funding that takes place with the closures of some of our national parks due to this virus. In a funny way, it will give everything within those boundaries an opportunity to breathe! We have a tendency to love the outdoors to death!

So, let me encourage you to lean into it. If you are new at it, do like Ruby. Maybe someone, a good partner or mentor, will have to help you restrain and release. If you are like Hope or me, getting a little slower athletically, use your leaning to stay active and be a mentor/helper. Pick up the birds as long as you can. Eventually, you will have to turn some of it over to fresh legs. We can make better decisions based off history even in the face of change that we may know nothing about. We adjust as we go if we are engaged. Data information in qualitative and quantitative forms is only as good as the engagement it creates. Today, March 28, 2020, we are three months in, give or take a few days, to the COVID-19 (according to the media). That short history has established a pattern that we are learning from. We are also looking back to other viral challenges through history to help with the present situation.

Never be afraid to admit you may be, or you were wrong on some issue. We make decisions based on the best info we have at the time. Allow others a pass if they miss the mark. Next time, get it on the first bounce by working together. Sometimes things are out of your control for immediate change, but that doesn't mean you take your ball and bat and go home. Sometimes sitting the bench and observing for an inning or two is a good thing. You will be a better contributor when you get back in the game.

Chapter 24

RUBY, GEM OF BALANCE

I WONDERED WHY RUBY EXHIBITED SUCH precise talents as we trained. After all, she was what the purist paper-focused dog breeder might call a freak of nature. I noticed things early on. Like how she watched, how she used her nose. How she paid attention when you talked to her. This dog had more going on than the mistake I may have labeled her when I listened too long to the crowd and so-called experts.

So, one day I asked my daughter, "Who did you say you got that yellow dog from in Clarkston?"

"Dad, I got her from a girl I worked with, and they live in Weston, Idaho." (The communities are close in proximity. My bad for not listening the first time.)

"What was her last name?" I asked.

"King," she said.

Then it hit me! Could it be?

She was digging for a picture on her phone. "This is them," and she turned the phone to me.

Well, I'll be dammed! Brent King! That name brought me this vision. I saw a Honda 70 (1972 model year) with Brent's dad balancing it, running alongside of it as they navigate up through the timber. This was the second time I bumped into them in the woods, and both times had elk in common. Brent was running along behind, trying to balance the back half of the elk that was draped over the seat! Brent couldn't have been much older than twelve years old.

The King family is part of my hometown history. Brent's father owned an auto body shop. His uncle DeVerl was a railroader. What they had in common with me was they were related to my latchkey sitter through Brent's mother's side—Elaine and Vern Smith (remember the shorthair Heidi in an earlier chapter). The Kings were hunters. They were not bird dog enthusiasts at that time, to my best recollection. I remember them as bowhunters. They were bowhunters who actually took game from time to time in those earlier days of bowhunting, using the more difficult-to-use equipment prior to the more complex mechanical ones so popular today. They were members of the local archery club, the Bear Lake Bowmen. I hung around that group as an inquisitive teenager, hoping to learn something about hunting with a bow and arrow.

Brent's father, Laver, was the first bowhunter I ever saw shoot at a big game animal in the field. We just happened to bump into each other about the time the elk did. I was fifteen years old and about twenty yards from this cow elk. I didn't know she was there, but I'd just spotted Laver and watched him shoot. Then all hell broke loose, and here came the cow! She burned by me at about ten yards, and I promptly shot in front of her. Then I noticed the arrow in her. Brent has a sister who is my age. Her name is Maurine. Her name is spelled exactly like my mother's. Maurine was a bit of an envy and ego smasher to the hunting group of fellers who participated in that outdoor effort in our high school. There were not allot of elk in those days. Rifle tags were a hard draw. Few of us who drew had shot one. Maurine found it prudent to shoot one, a large male elk that hunters refer to as a "Royal." Other than to acknowledge that it happened, none of them wanted to talk about it. I wanted to know every detail. After all, it was an elk for crying out loud! I can remember exactly where we were sitting in Ms. Burdick's English class as she told me the story.

Brent and I bumped into each other years later when we had our kids out fishing the same reservoir one spring day. And the discussion turned to dogs somehow. He mentioned he was raising Labs, and in the conversation, I remember it turning to recovery dogs, as in rescue dogs. And as I recall, they were getting a reputation and going at a premium price just south of four digits back then.

So, I have this reject of a yellow Lab that is an escape artist with a black tail. To top it off, she is wired for sound, as they say. Brent has an accounting practice in Logan, Utah, and lives twenty-five minutes north in Idaho. I ran him down to get the lowdown on Ruby. True. Dogs in Ruby's line have been purchased and are working search and rescue in California. That would make sense because Brent's father and uncle were way involved in search and rescue in the Bear Lake Valley. I guess I missed the part that Brent hunts the dog lines a bunch both upland and waterfowl.

Then I got a lesson in breeding and partnering for all the right reasons. Truly, Ruby was a "woops" and was from brother and sister of two different batches from the same parents. That is why she couldn't be registered. I had also learned, prior to this discussion, that some breeders will crossbreed intentionally, papers be damned, to keep certain characteristics in the line. I get it. My horses were all mustangs adopted from the Bureau of Land Management Wild Horse adoptions program. Those horses are mixtures not so well planned. I didn't have a sloppy mountain horse in the bunch. They did have papers from the BLM saying they belonged to me, but that was about it.

Most registered quarter horse owners look at you funny, out of one eye though, when you tell them they are mustangs. Even though their partial horse equine history is most likely tied to the creation of the mustang herds we now have if you could follow the lines back to the Great Depression when folks just turned out their horses due to the economics of it all. And it is odd that no quarter of a horse owner has ever been able to tell me what the other three-quarters of their horse was. It is a good thing there isn't a quarter dog association. I would be a mess.

Brent asked me if I'd heard of Snake River Retrievers out of the Idaho Falls, Idaho, area. I had. I knew they had a reputation of producing good hunting dogs here in this region. Well, it turns out that Ruby's grandfather is Seasides Casey Jones, and her great-grandfather is NFC/FC/AFC Dewey's Drake of Moon Rivers. For those of you who are into that following and understand the genetic importance, here is the list of outcomes by Drake:

- Two amateur wins at thirty months
- AFC title before age three

- AFC title at age four
- FC title age four
- Eleven all-age wins at six
- Number 5 on the 2002 High Points open list
- 2002 High Point Yellow Lab
- Qual. National Amateur 2001, 2002, 2003, 2004
- Qual. National Open 2002, 2003, 2004; National Amateur Finalist 2004
- 2004 National Field Champion

Sometimes you just get lucky! So, I'll take it. I look forward to continued good days with Ruby. With one year in the field, she has already shown good promise. She is a good conversation contributor with that off-colored tail. She would have gotten the chance to succeed even without this additional knowledge about her, because they all have gotten a chance. It is interesting to note the information though. Good information kind of works into the faith of it all.

I have worked alertly to not set her expectations against Hope's skills. I won't allow this new knowledge to cloud that. I already had her headed down her own path. I was looking through some old video of her first year. I wasn't sure she would ever learn to swim. Hope was swimming at three months like a beaver. Ruby had a delayed introduction to water. I have a great boat ramp that I worked her off of to begin with. But it was always in the back of my mind that she resembled someone in the throes of drowning. We kept at it. She wanted that bumper way more than the water was a deterrent. By fall, I was considering finding someone who could use her in dock dog competitions. She had developed wings and fins. The lesson: we both wanted it. That is the beginning of positive outcomes.

Forward to December 2020. By the time Ruby had returned the first mallard from the river, the second one was just above the rapids flowing down and around the bend and into the next slower stretch of the river. By the time I'd set Ruby up, the bird was a part of the rapids sixty yards off and gaining distance while being hid in the run by the turbulence. I dropped my hand in front of her nose, gave her the line, and said, "Back!" She reached the top of the run and then stopped and looked back for direction. I threw a big ten o'clock hand signal with another "Back."

Down the rapids she went, swimming around the corner and out of sight. I recalled the first time Hope disappeared there and the flood of concern that came with it. It felt the same. The run was familiar territory and old hat for Hope now after floating it I don't know how many times over the years. But this was a different dog, and she was faced with a new challenge. Somewhere around a minute, I thought maybe I should breathe. It was under three minutes, but they felt like hours, when I first spotted the yellow form coming through the brush, along the bank and upriver. The bonus was when she hit the opening on the point, I could see the mallard dangling from her mouth. Was that moment worth the effort, time, worry, and money? Not just yes but hell yes! She ran on faith, and we both were rewarded!

Chapter 25

A Better Place!

Earth Day, April 22, 2020

OGS HAVE TAUGHT ME ABOUT the effort involved in not moving too fast. What appears to be true at the time maybe isn't. When you start peeling off layers, you get closer to understanding the completeness of what it was you were peeling. It may be an onion clear to the core, but maybe you were expecting a usable core, and when you get there, it was soft and wormy. Are not you glad now that you just didn't chuck it whole in the stew? It could be that we as humans buy off on too many first-glance perceptions that something is true. The internet and the garbage pumped out of Facebook and Twitter often bark that messaging. Often, credibility is given to issues stated as fact, by those whose paths we may not know. I think we have some social responsibility to research best we can before we buy in to things that may impact the greater good. Then at least you made a choice with the best information available. Voting leaps to mind as something we too often don't do enough digging into before we cast our support. And then there is this statement: it is a secured sight. Nope. For everyone securing one, someone with evil intentions is un-securing another. Yet the greater good is used to force us all there. It is to the point that you almost cannot function without a computer or cell phone. And why are we forced there? Chew on that thought for a while.

Finished? How about this question: when was the last time you heard of a physical bank robbery that cleaned out a vault and several folks' life's savings? Now in the blink of an eye, a person's lifetime of savings can be whisked away electronically. Sit. Stay. Save your life!

As our public lands continue to be loved to death (thank you, Google Earth, not!), the survival of those open public lands, and the use opportunities for you and others, will continue to be put to votes in direct and indirect ways. So let me encourage you to better understand why those areas are there and visit them with more respect. Give back in some way. Help them find balance. If you want a simple project for the family, get some gloves and garbage sacks and go pick up litter on BLM, state, and forest lands. For the most part, it is easy to identify litter and easy to do. For the life of me, I just can't understand littering. Sure, something might blow out of an open pickup bed that you forgot to secure. To hold in your possession an item of trash, and then to toss it for others to look at and deal with drives me fast past the give passage opportunity of making a mistake. The forty-three beer cans I picked up last weekend out in the duck marsh hadn't been left there by ducks. I'm pretty sure it wasn't a solitude-seeking canoeist either. It was unfortunately someone from *my* recreational hobby crowd. Stop! Take up bowling. Leave the marsh. You are not responsible enough to be there. Intentional littering goes deep to unveil what you are about as a creature. You are really just all about you and no one else. You deserve to be included of just yourself. And you may need professional help because you are out of balance. And what is most disturbing is you most likely don't care!

Public lands are gems. Like a Ruby or Chips, we should work to help buff them up, to allow the best they have to offer come forth and then remain. Put a shine on them, so to speak. It will take constant attention. The selfish part of getting the most out of public lands isn't selfish at all, because with proper care and attention, everyone wins. That is balance! We should work to strike a balance. Chip's balance and shine came when I woke up and stopped pounding a square peg in a round hole. By pulling pheasant off her list of things thrust upon her by her appearance, we both enjoyed life more. I will most likely never experience grouse hunting again like Chips helped provide as I let her be Chips. That was a valuable life lesson she taught me beyond the activity of the hunt. It's OK to just be good at one thing. We can't know all things. Therefore, we cannot be perfect in all things, but we can contribute where we can. If you can do nothing more than be a good citizen, then you have contributed positively. The COVID-19 mess created messes we never knew existed. It also put those things on the map for change toward the positive. Many people have started the processes already. I was checked by a mask-wearing Department of Natural Resources officer at the boat launch the other day, and I was thankful I was. Thankful they showed up. It took one text to start the movement. Quagra Muscle infestation is a waterway (viral-like) pandemic (Google it.) So, yeah, for technology—balance it! Those needing an outlet from COVID-19 flocked to the river launches with everything that would float. And while there was a minimal risk that some boat or water toy this early in the year had floated in a muscle-contaminated muscle waterway, and then transported it here, the place is now on the map, and the shear amount of people learning about and using the place increases the risk of the muscle contamination into the future.

Citizens need to get in the social discussions in a way that works toward harmony of life and earth balance. Asking questions isn't illegal. Solutions won't come overnight, and they won't be easy to obtain. Questioning shouldn't get you fired. If it does, stand up and use the channels to fix it as soon as you can. It's hard to fight off wickedness on an empty stomach. If you're a corporation causing issues, guess what? You are made up of citizens, and some don't have stock in the company. You don't just have responsibility to the stockholder. You have a responsibility to everyone and everything that your brand or brands may touch, both for good and bad. You are out there and now responsible! Safe harbor laws exempt you from way too much responsibility to my way of thinking. Being honest would be a cost savings in the legality of it all, if nothing else.

If a newscast mentions the same word twice, it changes the Dow, and then that is news for today. It isn't often the negative or positive impacts of tomorrow. The media regurgitates what it sees, taking less and less time to dig in because it may hurt the ratings and sponsorships of the outlet and their financial supporters. PR spin doctors create "truth" from half-truth and blatant lies. The bean counters are in control because they may have a mortgage. Most of the time, the bean counters unfortunately have CEOs who just make way too much money for their contributions to life by giving marching orders that are self-serving. The noise and confusion they create by pounding square pegs in a round hole chokes the life out of good contributions.

Lasting brands show good social leadership. They take on difficult conversations. They don't stick their heads in the sand and hope no one notices. They show up. They admit they don't have all the answers. They are willing to place the time and effort to acquire honest and effective social solutions. They cannot speak with a forked tongue. The information age is helping the public who want to become more educated quickly. Don't send your PR folks to a partnering organization's function only to have them badmouth the group they are supposed to be supporting to another brand that is at the event. It's a small world. But maybe you just didn't peel the onion enough. Still, that is your bad! Then again, maybe they just knew how to write a good résumé (lie) to get around the hiring algorithm. Now they are a worm in your onion.

My hope and faith are that my dog partners continue to help me get to a better place. And that I can better contribute positively from being there. Dogs are honest. They get confused and don't perform when you, as the other partner, are mixing signals. You have screwed up. I have screwed up. Admit it, apologize, grow from it, change course, and move forward. I'm well aware of the fingers pointing back at me, as I've pointed a finger in this writing at others and the personal responsibility that comes from that type of sign language.

As a kid, when I got a bit out of line, or I did something contrary to parental guidance, my father used to say, "I have a bone to pick with you." So I want to leave you with a bone to pick on. What does it mean, and what do you have to do, to make the world honestly a better place? It is not enough to say, "It's going to the dogs." What does that mean anyway? Maybe it should go to the dogs for the simple truth that they are always honest.

POSTSCRIPT, DECEMBER 2020

A book needs to end somewhere, and I'd thought I'd found that ending. But life continued to move it. There was a bit of delay finding photographs. Early slides I'd made into prints for albums. They needed electronic submission. So I took photos of those to use in the book. Sorry if they were not clearer, but photography has changed a bunch in fifty years. Zip drives contained other more recent photos that my computer wouldn't load, and my human retriever of such items became waylaid by the pandemic, as did others who needed to influence this manuscript.

My publishing company has also had a few minor setbacks that delayed this getting to book form and publication, but they were stellar in communication, support, and encouragement.

While the photographs have been the biggest delay, that delay has allowed me time to observe accuracy and inaccuracies of some opinions in this writing. Most likely, those observations deserve another book. But the media seems to have the release of books well at hand as they pertain to all things pandemic and political.

I would, however, like to thank the Utah Division of Workforce Services. My experience with them because of the pandemic and prior layoff has helped me practice more patience, compassion, and understanding with Hope, my aging Lab. At age eleven, which is seventy-seven in dog years, she is still getting it done. Her sight and hearing are going. Her nose is still keen. I work to provide positive experiences for her at her age and give her the respect she deserves. I don't change the rules midstream on her, and I apologize when I screw up. All her knowledge has allowed her to be an excellent mentor for Ruby and, oddly enough, some hunters in the field. We are here because she was there. There is value in age. UDWFS should try to find out what it is. Maybe bundle that discovery into a meaningful service work opportunities for the senior working class who either need to or choose to work in their later years. But first they need to figure out how to get rid of the discriminatory algorithms used in hiring practices by the employers they also try to support. By ignoring it, they support age discrimination. Partners in crime ... maybe? Maybe it is just the issue of a mortgage and car payments to those in charge. Certainly, I spoke with more than one disgruntled government employee stuck between doing the right thing and policies that no longer fit the current life situations of many who the UDWFS is supposed to *serve*. Government programs too often are like Chip's relationship with me early on—square pegs and round holes.

National and state parks closed early in the pandemic, saved a dime, then got run over once they opened from folks being pent up by the pandemic, desiring to get out and do something, anything. Here on our forest lands, we trampled accessible places to dust. Forty-eight primitive-style campsites popped to the surface along a watershed over the summer. The Forest Service reduced them to twenty-three using rock barricades. We seem to lack the ability to govern ourselves in a manner outdoors that isn't intrusive to the health of the resources. We seem to have time to abuse it but not engage and maintain it. Complaining is not a positive contribution. Decisions are made by those who show up. Those folks we have hired to do it follow their own algorithms. I suggest we all reengage. The outdoor ethic becomes cloudier each day we don't.

I've not seen the marshes and rivers as crowded as I have this past summer and fall. Social distancing and lockdowns have driven folks to the outdoors. Outdoors is a big place. But handy places outdoors are taking a beating. Time will tell the colors of the outdoor industry to see if they take the social responsibility of helping fix land and water impacts created by the use of the toys they create and distribute to help folks overrun the outdoors. The excise tax on some hunting and fishing gear under the Pittman Robertson and Dingell Johnson Acts continues to lead the way of contributing and paying back for usage outdoors. And not to overburden the sportsman with taxation, but what about a similar tax on other items used outdoors? If the word *tax* bothers you, then call it a donation.

By the time this book hits the shelves, many small businesses in the food world will be gone. Please work to support those that are left. Those folks truly work hard for the money. While a picnic atop a log or rock is a great experience, maybe plan your schedule to eat breakfast or dinner at a local mom-and-pop eatery on the way out and back. That is, if you can still find one whose doors are open. While traveling during my careers, I often sought out these places for a quiet breakfast or lunch. You want to learn about an area you visit? Eat where the locals do and listen. You'll get the pulse of America.

Our first responders, service workers, health professionals, law enforcement, and military, tell them thank you and mean it! I had thirty-three different nurses while recovering from my heart surgery. Only one might not have continued in the profession, but she was swinging at it best she could. I believe some of it is a gift bestowed upon them when they choose that occupation. On two separate occasions, nurses noticed something not right in my recovery and shifted my direction. One gal was going through a divorce, had four kids, and was working nights. On the fly and out of the corner of her eye, she noticed I had a drain issue with a lung. Two hours later, thirty-two ounces of fluid had been removed so I could continue to heal. That's a Big Gulp from 7-11. My surgeon who I'd never met prior but was going to open me up in ten hours was a fly fisherman. That allowed me to relax some. And really, I hated having to suggest we can the storytelling and he should go home, get a meal, kiss the wife, and get a good night's rest before he cut into me the next morning. My daughter-in-law is a bit of a vampire and is now over the blood work at a county hospital. The COVID virus itself is real. Some of the numbers and death coding may be inaccurate due to our human selves. But the efforts created and lives upset by COVID are real. Abuse of the pandemic to take intentional advantage of others is immoral! The pandemic certainly has flushed out what was in the brush pile of society, and I may have finally found the end to this writing. It is directed to some of our politicians. "Bad human." My dogs know who feeds them. Need I remind some of you who feeds you? We, like dogs, whisper, so ... listen up!

Me, Duke, and my Brother

Hunting duds

Sage chicken's

Mom Dolly

Dolly at work

The results

Pup Star

We dig boats

Push it up!

Your who?

1-100, 2-100, 3-100

Bena's snow play

A long runner

Rena, An unbelievable Pleasure to hunt behind.
I lost only one bird over her, a long flyer that died
in tule well. She never caught live birds. She'd hold point
till the bird left. She was a tracker. She'd hand signal
and blinker retrieve. The Record was 95 roosters shot
over her in one year on public land. thanks
Girl

Cocoa- youth mentor

Mountain birds

Coke and Ri same place 8 years later

Maggie, Hope, Coke

Exercises kennel

Hope-ten weeks

Building the blind

Dang metal!

40 years prior Dolly sat on Hopes spot

Labs do Ruffys

Entertaining accounts

More business

Snows

Mike and Quinney

Josh and queen Teal

Cove

Got Goose?

A higher power

Goose ghost

Hope and Mom

"In my space, really?"

Grump slump

Rooster rooter

"I do what?"

Pallet fire slobs

Learning the big swims

River watch

The amazing Jack

Team Work

Spud

No free lunch

Special thanks to John and Grant White for working to keep an open space for dogs to build Humans.

Sportsman's Paradise
www.whitesranch.com
goodtrout@aol.com

Printed in the United States
by Baker & Taylor Publisher Services